OUT OF [
INTO
LIGHT

TRUE-TO-LIFE STORIES OF

MUSLIMS COMING TO JESUS CHRIST

THROUGH DREAMS, VISIONS & MIRACLES

COMPILED BY:

ALI ABDEL MASIH

PUBLISHED BY:

MGB PRINTING SERVICES INC.

TO ORDER BOOKS GO ONLINE TO

www.outofdarknessintolight.com

ISBN: 978-0-9832294-2-1

INDEX

INTRODUCTION

ALI ABDEL MASIH

I lived in the U.S. for most of my life. It was here I came to know the Lord. Out of the darkness and emptiness of religion, I came to know a Living God Who fills the hearts of all who seek Him with joy and life indescribable.

Soon after I met the Lord, I began listening to a radio program called *Readers Choice*. They read books from cover to cover. I loved the program and listened religiously. Few books touched me as deeply as one called *The Jackrabbit Preacher*. The author was anonymous. He said his identity wasn't central to the message of God's unflinching grace that he sought to expound. The sermons contained in the book lifted me to heaven and helped me grasp the message of grace like no other. Might it have been because my mind wasn't distracted by the identity of the writer? I don't know.

This book is the same in that my identity isn't that important. I could easily say who I am and not fear repercussions. The stories I tell are true. These are real people who live in lands where they could die if their identity were revealed. In fact, if my identity were known, their connection to me could endanger them. So, for more reasons than one, I'll just call myself Ali Abdel Masih.

In Islam, someone who leaves his religion is supposed to be killed, though there are very few people who would carry out this sentence. It is prescribed in the Koran,

"If they forsake you, pursue them and kill them wherever you find them."

FOLLOWING THE LIGHT

Jesus said that those who are led of the Spirit are like the wind. I have traveled and lived in many of the hardest places in the world in terms of receptivity to the Gospel. In that darkness, I saw God's light shine so brilliantly that I often had to look away.

When something exciting happens in our lives our first reaction is to look for someone to share it with. We usually look for those who are closest to us and who we know will rejoice with us. It will encourage us, but perhaps more importantly, it will encourage our listeners.

SHARING TESTIMONIES

I wanted to share these testimonies with America first. I love America, not only because I was born and raised here, but because in all my travels I have come to believe in American exceptionalism. This exceptionalism is not just because we are the greatest economic powerhouse in the world. It is because of our spiritual heritage. The cynics are snickering, I know. Let them snicker. Though dogs bark, the moon shines on in brightness. Having seen how people struggle and suffer in the world, I believe that being an American is a gift. I believe I was granted by God to be American so that I could come and go. It's so easy to get sidelined defending my beloved America—I won't. It was in America that I, as a young Muslim, met Jesus Christ. His glorious light filled my heart here.

Afterward that, I felt a need to go back to my brothers and sisters still in the darkness that I once knew and share with them this light. When I did, I was amazed, not so much by the responses of the people. I wasn't even amazed by the strength I found in myself to endure hardships that such a calling entails. I was amazed, however, at the way the God of Abraham was so eager to demonstrate His truth to and through me, as well as to and through anyone who would allow Him.

PROPELLED BY HIS GRACE

This book is about Him and what He does. It is in obedience to God's command in Psalms 96 that we declare His mighty works. He is the Wind. I'm like the tumbleweed that is driven by this Wind. I was irresistibly propelled by His grace. That same gale propels all believers wherever they are and wherever they serve. If we trust Him to lead, He will.

REACHING THE SONS AND DAUGHTERS OF ISHMAEL

We especially need to learn His ways in reaching the sons and daughters of Ishmael who are our neighbors, friends, relatives, and co-workers. You can't liberate people from harsh religion with more harsh religion. If we become hardened in our views toward these for whom the Son of God died, we will lose them. But if we uproot ourselves from our rights, privileges, and perceived injustices, as He did to reach us, we will reach them. He left the throne of glory to be clothed in the stench of fallen humanity and to bear in His humanity our ugliness to the full. We need to do the same for Him and for them. When we do, they will see through us to the One Whose wind propels us toward them in this furious, hurricane force, gale of grace.

My prayer today is that when you open the pages of this book you will begin to see the difference between the religions of the world such as Christianity, Islam, Buddhism, etc., and becoming a child of God.

I have found that religion in and of itself has no life, no peace, no love, no joy, no forgiveness, and no hope. Religion is dead; it offers these attributes but in the end only delivers death, because there is no life in religion. Religion, including the "religion" of Christianity, is part of the kingdom of darkness.

You see, there are only two kingdoms at work in this world: the kingdom of darkness and the Kingdom of Light. Jesus is the King of the Kingdom of Light and Satan is the king of the kingdom of darkness. The very definition of religion is, simply put, "witchcraft," based on fear, intimidation, manipulation, domination, and control. Jesus,

Who is also called Wonderful Counsellor, Mighty God, Everlasting Father, and the Prince of Peace, does not practice witchcraft. We all know who does.

Written within these pages are true stories, or "testimonies" as I am calling them, which will bring you to life if you will only stop and listen to what King Jesus is saying to you through them. The Christianity described and written within these pages is not the *dead* religion you hear of today. It is rather *true* Christianity, as meant to be expressed according to God's Holy Word, the Bible. True Christianity is not a *religion*; rather, it is a *relationship*, a Father to child relationship. Jesus is quoted in the Holy Bible:

> *And Jesus called a little child unto him, and set him in the midst of them, And said, Verily I say unto you, Except ye be converted, and become as little children, ye shall not enter into the kingdom of heaven. Whosoever therefore shall humble himself as this little child, the same is greatest in the kingdom of heaven.* (Matthew 18:2-4)

Jesus says that we must become a child of God to enter into His Kingdom. The true stories in this book are those who have become children of the Most High God coming *Out of Darkness into Light* by the power of God the Holy Spirit, as described in the Holy Bible:

vii

But as many as received him [Jesus], to them gave he power to become the sons of God, even to them that believe on his name: Which were born, not of blood, nor of the will of the flesh, nor of the will of man, but of God. (John 1:12-13)

The Holy Bible also states that when anyone turns toward the Lord Jesus Christ, the veil is lifted or taken away, and we begin to see and then break free from the kingdom of darkness into the Kingdom of Light.

But their minds were blinded: for until this day remained the same veil untaken away in the reading of the old testament; which veil is done away in Christ. But even unto this day, when Moses [Old Testament] is read, the veil is upon their heart. Nevertheless when they shall turn to the Lord, the veil shall be taken away. Now the Lord is that Spirit: and where the Spirit of the Lord is, there is liberty. (2 Corinthians 3:14-17)

The stories you are about to read are true—this is what happened to us. When we turn to the Lord Jesus Christ the veil of darkness is lifted, and then we are brought out of the *darkness* into the *light*.

Enjoy.

1

THE TESTIMONY
OF AHMED

I was always the fighter. I was quiet, contemplative, and friendly for the most part, but once my fuse was lit I might do anything. I was uncontrollable, you might say. My family knew this, my friends knew this, and most of all, I knew it about myself.

I was a soldier of the highest rank. I didn't belong to a national army; we were mostly guerrilla fighters. My size and strength made me valuable to my commanders. I knew how to give and take orders, and I was ready to die for what I believed in.

I was progressing and surpassing my peers in almost every way. Everything was going along fine with me until, one day, I went to an accounting class that was being taught by an American named Tom. He was also Arab, I think, and he spoke with a halting, back-hills Arabic dialect. I knew he was a Christian, but it didn't matter. I liked him and was drawn to his personality and teaching style. He often made the students laugh. I only attended the class twice, but I couldn't get it out of my mind.

The second time I attended, he told us he was going to be singing and playing piano at a meeting. He told us it was the American holiday of Thanksgiving. It would give us, if we wanted, a chance to meet other people who spoke English.

I wanted to go but was so torn. I didn't like the way I was drawn to Tom; I really admired him, even though he was a Christian. I had always been a strict Muslim. My family even had plans to train me as an Imam.

On the night of the concert, I told some friends to come with me. The meeting was in a large wedding hall. I saw Tom from afar. I didn't want to go in so I stayed outside. My friends went in and called me to join them. I finally went in. The music was in Arabic, and it was about Jesus. People were lifting their hands and singing along. I saw Tom playing. I felt a great peace in my heart like I had never known before. It was so powerful, and I was terrified. I ran out of the building. My friends followed me later.

I went home. I was sweating bullets and couldn't concentrate. Nothing mattered in the world except knowing what I was feeling at the meeting. I tossed and turned in my bed until I finally fell asleep.

Then the dreams began. I saw a Man who didn't speak to me or even look at me, but I knew He was there because of me and as a message to me. That much I knew.

Who was He? The whole night passed like a single second. I woke up still sweating.

I couldn't stop thinking about my dream. What did it mean? Who was that man?

After breakfast with my family, I went to college. I tried to focus on my classes. One of the lessons was about Islam's superiority to Christianity. The speaker spoke angrily and yet persuasively. It was so different from what I had felt the night before.

After school, I went to my usual military drills. I was a leader, and I had to keep tabs on my soldiers. They all looked up to me. I knew my soldiers looked at me with fear and intimidation because of my size and strength, but I couldn't have felt any smaller than I felt now. Everything I believed and was fighting for seemed so small and insignificant now. Everyone noticed the change in me.

I tried to pretend everything was fine, but it got to the point that my superiors noticed the difference in me and started complaining. They told me I had been working too much and that I needed some time off. They told me to take two weeks off. All I could do, I thought, was to put it out of my mind and get back to my studies.

I was exhausted by nightfall. I usually go to sleep early, but today I didn't even eat dinner. The outward pressure was nothing compared to the inner stress I was feeling. I was so tired that I just went to my room, collapsed on my mattress, and fell into a deep sleep.

That Man!!! He was there again!!! I just stared at Him. He didn't speak. He didn't even look at me. He just stood there, but I knew He was there for me and because of me. What did he want? I know He knew I was looking at Him, but I wasn't afraid of Him. I knew He wouldn't hurt me, and I knew He cared for me and wanted me.

I awoke to the sound of the call to prayer and got ready to go to the mosque, but it felt so empty. It was always empty, but it was emptier now. It was just movements and words: kneel, stand up, put my hand on my stomach, look to the right, look to the left, kneel again, chant, and mumble; it was the same words over and over.

After prayer I went home, but I was still tired. I slept until my mother woke me up for breakfast. I ate and hurried out of the house. Even though I had classes to attend, I didn't care. I just wanted to find someone who could tell me who the Man was in my dreams was. I looked around but couldn't find anyone. I felt helpless. I wasn't sure if I could find Tom. The classes had ended, and I thought he might have returned to America.

The dreams continued, night after night after night. I came to expect them, in fact. I even started looking forward to them. It gave me a sense of security to know that this Man would be there every night. Then, one night, after several months, the dreams stopped.

He wasn't there.

I was terrified. I didn't know if I had done something to anger Him. I didn't know if He was angry because I didn't get a Bible or talk to Christians to find out more about Him. I didn't know for sure Who He was or what the dreams or their cessation meant, but I was terrified. I didn't know what to do or who to talk to. There were no churches in our town. I would have to go to the big city to ask a priest about what happened.

The next day, I went to the city and found a church. My family is very well known, and some of the people in the church were afraid of me. They wouldn't talk to me. I told them that I needed to understand about Jesus, but no one would help me. I was so scared that I would never see the Man in my dreams again. Why did He leave me? Who was He?

Finally, I felt I had no choice but to go see if Tom was still around. I found him teaching his class. I waited until he was finished. He looked at me, but he clearly didn't recognize me. I told him that I had attended his class a few months earlier.

"Welcome," he said.

"I need to talk to you," I said.

We went out for coffee and sat in a corner away from all the ruckus in the café. He looked at me intently. I think he could see how scared I was. "What's up? What happened?" he asked.

I tried to find the words, but it was so hard. My thoughts rushed in from a million directions about the dreams, the feelings, the peace, the prayers, the priest, and everything that was happening. I finally just started by telling him about the dreams that started when I went to the meeting where he was playing and singing.

Without hesitation he said, "That's Jesus."

"I know," I said. "I had a feeling it was, but why did He come to me all those nights or all those months? What does He want from me? And why did He stop coming to me?"

Tom looked at me intently. I expected my story to shock him, but it seemed as if he understood exactly what was happening to me, almost as if he had heard it before.

"I don't know why they stopped, but I know why they started," Tom said, and he proceeded to tell me the Gospel story. He told me what Jesus had done for us in dying on the cross.

The words he spoke were like a water fountain. It was as if the dreams created in me a thirst that I've lived with all these months.

I eagerly prayed with Tom to accept the Lord. I felt the light was turned on inside my heart. The darkness was gone. I just stared at Tom with the look of a satisfied man. I was so satisfied. I had looked for this satisfaction for so long. I thought I'd find it in my strength, but instead I found it in this deepest place of brokenness and humility.

Tom started teaching me about the Bible once a week. I would secretly go to his house where we would study. I was devouring the lessons. We also sang. I loved the songs and memorized them.

My whole life changed. I even quit my military training. My commanders came by and tried to get me to go back with them, but I couldn't. Neither could I tell them that I had become a Christian. They were becoming suspicious, however, that something had happened in me. Some even started following me around, but I didn't care. I knew I had found the greatest treasure in the universe, and that no one could take it away from me.

One day, Tom was gone on a journey, and I was alone in the city. It was a Friday, and I felt so alone. I knew that people were following me. I didn't know what to do, so I just walked to the park. I sat on a bench and put my head in my palms. Tears streamed from my eyes.

"How could I continue to live like this?" I wondered. "My whole future is doomed if anyone finds out. I can't live a lie like this, but I can't tell them the truth."

The thoughts and the loneliness were tormenting me. Then I looked up. In the distance I saw a man. He was standing at the far end of the park. He was just looking at me and smiling. He waved at me, and I felt that same peace I had felt that first night. I rubbed my eyes and looked again, and he was gone. My heart started jumping for joy. I knew the Lord was with me. I knew he was with me before, but now I knew it for real. Nothing could shake my faith even if I were alone.

I wanted to tell people about my faith, but it was so hard in our strictly Islamic community. My father was a great man and well respected in the community. He was faithful to his family and his mosque. Even though he was open-minded, I didn't know how he would react when he found out his oldest son was a Christian.

My family noticed that I stopped going to the mosque. They tried to find out why. I didn't know what to tell them.

To get them to stop pressuring me, I decided to go to the mosque just once. I did all the right movements, but under my breath I was praying to Jesus. After kneeling and bowing my head to the ground I raised my head from the prayer rug. For an instant, I saw Jesus in front of me wiping the sweat off my forehead. I knew then that there was nowhere I could go that He wasn't with me.

Such joy welled up inside of me that I could hardly contain it. I wanted to tell someone. I called Tom after the prayer. He was overjoyed as well. I knew that this vision meant there was no turning back for me. I didn't want to turn back, but it would also be harder to pretend I was still a Muslim.

Eventually, all would know that I had become a Christian. I wanted so badly for that day to arrive. But I had to consider the impact on my family and the other believers, so I bided my time.

After months of hiding my faith, I told my family everything. Their reaction was as I expected. They kicked me out of the house. They begged me not to tell anyone because it would be a great source of shame to the family.

I started sleeping in the streets. I had to be careful where I stayed and slept because members of the military were still looking for me. If they caught me, I feared they would kill me.

One time, I was actually apprehended by some members of my former squad. They knew about my Christianity and wanted me to deny Christ. They offered me money and a home. They told me I would have a secure future. I was so exhausted and felt so alone, but I couldn't deny Christ.

The springs of joy that welled up inside of me were so small sometimes, but they were there. I couldn't deny His presence in me. When the enticements didn't work, they tried beating me. They also tried different types of torture, which I won't discuss. I was imprisoned and judged. Because of my family, they wouldn't kill me. In the end, I was told not to tell anyone about my faith and I was released.

Expecting that they would try to kill me, I just started hiding. I found ways to get food, and I had some friends who secretly helped me.

I felt there was one step I needed to take to completely make a break with my past—baptism. I asked some of the brothers to baptize me. They all asked me to do it in a home, in a bathtub, but I wanted it to be out in a public place. I suggested a nearby river.

When I decided to be baptized publicly, some of the other secret believers were also baptized. We went out to the river and were baptized in the Name of the Lord Jesus Christ, the Father, Son and Holy Spirit. I felt like a new man.

Almost immediately after the baptism, the persecution intensified. My soul sank into regions of darkness that I never knew existed. I was all alone for a long time and unable to meet with believers or even speak to anyone. I didn't even feel as if God were with me. It was the darkest time I had ever known.

I climbed a very high tree. Beneath the tree was a valley of jagged rocks. I wanted to jump off and go home to be with Jesus.

My loneliness and depression were so strong. As I neared the top of the tree, I asked God to forgive me. I wanted Him to understand how much pain I was in.

Then I saw a light on the tree with me. The Man in my dreams appeared. He said, "You are my son."

I wanted to cry, I was so overwhelmed by joy. Could he have been with me all these days and months? He was! I climbed down the tree and went back to my tent.

Arms of love were cradling me from beneath. I couldn't deny the glory. The pain and the glory seemed to go together, but the glory was greater. I cried alone and felt forsaken by the whole world, but the springs of life that had sustained me when I came to Christ have never stopped flowing in me.

2

THE TESTIMONY
OF ADEL

O
ur village is on a small hill in the shadow of our ancient capital. The Old City with its mosques and legends fills our minds with ancient mystique. My family made regular pilgrimages to the hallowed fonts and storied houses of worship.

My family was special this way. For many generations we were the leaders in the village mosque. My grandfather was one of the most respected leaders in our community. He was sharp, witty, and an excellent communicator.

My father, Mohammed, was the same. He seemed to possess that same uncanny ability to charm his listeners, while instilling them with hope and passion. People would often come and seek counsel from my father and grandfather. My uncles were also highly regarded in the mosque and community. I was different.

It just didn't click with me. I didn't know how to fit in with all the rest. I tried many times but felt awkward, empty, and out of place. It was, of course, expected that I would be like my father and grandfather.

Everything inside me rebelled against the idea. I didn't want to be like them. They seemed to me empty shells. People saw them as hallowed wise men, but I saw them as images—empty images. People love images, and they love to have people to put up on high pedestals. My family relished the opportunity to stand on those pedestals and be admired, respected, and sought out.

It drove me mad, and I felt an emptiness inside that gnawed at me day and night. I didn't want to be the next shiny image on the pedestal. I wanted some reality. They always talked about Allah, Islam, the Koran, and the stories of the great heroes. It kindled peoples' imaginations, filling them with awe and wonder.

It didn't affect me that way. I knew I couldn't be like them. Little by little, I began drifting away. I tried burying myself in my work. My father also owned an auto garage, and I worked for him as a mechanic. The work was gruelling, and the pay was low, but it was a great distraction from my inner turmoil.

As a teenager, after work I'd often sneak away to the Old City alone. Cities that are known for holy relics are also the best places to find all sorts of scarcely concealed temptations. For me, it was alcohol. I started drinking a little bit of beer with some of the young men around the city walls. We'd sit, drink, and laugh until we passed out or got sick. In the hustle and bustle of the Old City environs, no one ever seemed to notice me. No one knew that I was the son of one of their most respected religious leaders.

I didn't like what I was doing, but for some reason it felt more real to me than what I saw in my family. The stories, legends, and heroes were like peals of thunder that frightened us and kept us in our place, but in the end yielded no rain. To those outside it seemed like something more, but I was on the inside, and to me it felt like an illusion.

I started going to the Old City once or twice a week, but before long it was every day. I'd finish my work, get cleaned up, and head to the Old City. My family rarely saw me except around bedtime; even then, I was uncommunicative and despondent.

One day, as I was walking through the Old City on my way to a secluded bar, I noticed some people sitting around a television and watching a movie. I stood with them for a while. It was a movie about the Prophet Isa. I recognized him from pictures I had seen in the past: the long hair, the beard, and the white gown.

At first, I watched because I was bored, but eventually I found myself engrossed in the movie. I stood outside and watched the whole movie with them. I saw Isa open the eyes of the blind. I listened as He taught about love and forgiveness. I saw Him raise the dead. I had heard of all these things about Isa in the Koran; they were not new to me.

But then, I saw Him killed on the cross. The Koran, as we were taught, says he was not killed on the cross. It says, "They didn't kill him. They didn't crucify him, but it was made to look like it to them." We were taught that Allah took Isa into heaven and made someone else look like him. It was that *other* person who was crucified. I was always taught that it was Judas, the betrayer, who was crucified instead of Jesus.

When I saw this movie, it made sense that Jesus was the one who died and not Judas. Yet, as rebellious as I was, I wasn't ready to deny my Muslim faith and believe that it was actually Jesus who was crucified. One of the key teachings about Jesus in Islam is that He didn't die but was rescued by God at the last moment.

I thought about it often. The Christians also intrigued me. They seemed different from my family. They seemed happier and more peaceful. How could I be like that? I really wanted that peace and happiness. I had tried so many times to be a good religious person, but it didn't work. All I found was emptiness and misery.

I went to the bar and found my drinking buddies. We sat around drinking, but I wasn't laughing as much. They could tell that my thoughts were elsewhere. They asked me what was wrong, but I couldn't tell them. Even though they were drinking alcohol, which is a great sin in Islam, if I told them that I was interested in Christianity they would have instantly feigned religiosity. I didn't tell them, but I kept thinking about the movie, the Christians, and the happiness I saw.

My family began to notice the change in me. I was twenty years old now, and they wanted me to think about marriage, career, and religious instruction. I wasn't interested in any of it. I loved them so much, but I couldn't force myself to fit into their mold. My father took me to the mosque and tried to convince me to follow my family traditions, but I couldn't.

My only escape from the confusion and guilt was drinking. It became almost a daily thing with me now. I would sit outside the Old City, sometimes alone, and drink one beer after another.

One Monday afternoon, I was sitting with my beer bottle, alone, near the city gate. There was a nice seating area where the drunks usually gathered. I didn't want to be with anyone today. I often was like that. Maybe it was the guilt or selfishness; I didn't know what it was, but I liked being alone.

"Maybe this is all there really is to life," I thought repeatedly. It became like a song that I couldn't get out of my mind. I really wanted to abandon the thought but felt helpless to resist it. I was preoccupied by it. The darkness was worse than usual that day. The hopelessness was almost palpable. I was afraid that if I just let go, my emotions would sink deeper and deeper into despair.

I took an extra long swig and closed my eyes as the alcohol washed down my throat. I was hoping that when I opened my eyes I'd find that everything was just a dream. As I sat alone, a man came up to me. He was wearing a baseball cap and western clothes and was carrying a backpack. He was smiling.

"May I join you?" he asked in broken Arabic.

He looked Arab, but there was something different about him, too. He seemed friendly enough. I offered him some of my beer, but he refused. "I'm out telling people about Jesus. May I talk to you?" he asked. His name was Trevor. I was impressed by his boldness and, in all honesty, this was exactly what I was hoping for.

Without hesitation I asked him, "How can I live this life?"

He explained to me the message of the Gospel. He told me how Jesus came to earth to die for us. He told me that I couldn't live the life that God wants in my own strength. I needed to have the power of God in my heart first. I was amazed at his words.

When he asked me if I wanted to accept Jesus as my Savior, I instantly said, "Yes." We prayed a simple prayer, and he asked me how I felt.

"I feel like I'm flying," I told him. I threw away my beer bottle, as I knew that God didn't want me to keep drinking.

He seemed overjoyed at my decision and took me to meet a Christian friend of his, Zuhar, who worked in the Old City. Trevor lived many miles away and wouldn't be able to come see me everyday, so he wanted me to have other friends nearby with whom I could talk.

I started to read the Bible, and it filled me with such joy. I was full of expectancy. I came to meet Zuhar almost every day. I even started going to church with him. My spirit was growing, and I knew that I had found the truth.

Things were going well for me spiritually until my family found the small New Testament Zuhar had given me. My mother tried to protect me from my father's wrath, but it was useless. He yelled at me, as did my brothers. Even some of my cousins found out. It became unbearable for me. I went to look for Trevor but was unable to find him.

I needed to see someone to encourage me. I was terrified and unsure of what to do. I finally got in touch with Trevor, and we met in the Old City. He told me how he, too, had been a Muslim and had come to know Jesus. He said that his family disowned him, but he found great joy in a promise from the Bible:

And every one [who has given up] houses, or brothers, or sisters, or father, or mother, or wife, or children, or lands for my Name's sake, shall receive a hundredfold, and shall inherit everlasting life. (Matthew 19:29)

I was so happy to know that Trevor had also been a Muslim and that he understood what I was going through. I started calling him every day, and we became very good friends. The commotion in my family seemed to die down a little. I was able to go home, but no one talked to me. My mother was the only one who was really nice to me. I would have liked to leave, but I had no choice—I had nowhere else to go.

A few weeks later, during work, I was fixing a second story window at my father's garage. I was standing on a ladder when a car sped around the corner, rammed right into the ladder, and sped off. I fell and broke my right leg. I laid on the ground until my brother took me to the hospital. The pain was unbearable. I really wanted to have someone with me in the hospital room, but no one came. I didn't have my phone to call anyone, and not one member of my family came to see me. I was there for days alone.

The pain in my leg subsided, but the pain in my heart deepened as I realized that my family would never accept me as a Christian. In the sadness, I instinctively hung my head as a single tear fell from my eye onto the bed sheets. Then suddenly, it felt as if someone opened a window and let a fresh breeze in. I felt solace in my spirit. It was so deep and tangible. It felt like a gift that no one could ever take away. I looked around to see if anyone was there, but I could see no one with my eyes. Still, I knew someone was there with me—someone was there—Jesus. He, Whom I had accepted a few days before, was there with me. When I learned to know His presence, I realized that He had been with me the whole time.

With my leg in a cast and walking with a cane, I went to church a few weeks later. They gave a chance for people to share a testimony. I stumbled to my feet with a cane in one hand. I told them what had happened to me and how I had been in the hospital.

"Not one member of my family came to see me," I said. "But, I know someone was there with me!"

Yes, Jesus was with me and will always be with me.

3

THE TESTIMONY
OF ALI

I passed by the Bethel Church on my way home from school every day. The adobe-colored brick structure had a sharp, high-peaked ceiling and steeple, with a stained-glassed window the whole length of the wall. A 20-foot wooden cross was affixed to the façade.

Every time I walked by it, I would spit on the lawn right in front of the cross. It became almost a religious duty with me. Sometimes I looked around to make sure no one saw me, but most of the time I hoped they did.

"Didn't people know that these things were blasphemous?" I thought to myself. "Weren't they scared of going to hell?"

I, for one, was terrified of going to hell. My name is Ali. I was born in America but spent a good deal of my childhood in my father's homeland. There I attended school and learned Arabic and, more importantly, Islam.

I hated crosses. I would even avoid looking at telephone poles because they were in the shape of crosses. Like all good Muslims, I didn't eat ham or bacon. I would meticulously read the ingredients on food labels to make sure it didn't contain pork. If I didn't understand an ingredient I would look it up in the dictionary to make sure it wasn't pork.

Even though I hated things that represented Christianity, as I felt I should, I didn't hate Jesus. As a Muslim, I revered Him as the Prophet Isa in the Koran. He healed people and did wonders. The Koran says that He created a bird and spoke as a baby in the manger, "Peace be upon me in the day I am born, the day I die, and the day I am returned to life."

Although I loved Jesus, I was a Muslim and knew my primary allegiance was not to Jesus but to Mohammed. I believed Mohammed was the last messenger who was sent to restore the truth after evil men corrupted the holy books.

I was born in the U.S. Like many of his countrymen, my father had left his Arab homeland and traveled to South America. He met my Mother, they married, and traveled to the U.S. where I was born. Even though she was Catholic, it was decided by them both that I would be raised a Muslim.

As a youth in the U.S., I never really knew Islam. Although we were culturally Muslim, my father was illiterate and knew little about his religion.

The only time I went inside a church was when a friend of ours got married and she asked that I be the ring bearer. As I walked down the aisle of the church, I kept staring at pictures portraying the Stations of the Cross. It was mesmerizing to me. Then, I saw a huge painting of

Jesus with two fingers raised in blessing. I stared at it for a long time. I loved Him.

I wanted to know about Jesus. I had seen movies and the terrifying scenes of crucifixion: the nails, the whips, the blood, the mobs, and the rage. I also remembered the miracles, the love, and the forgiveness.

When I was seven years old, because of my constant pestering, my mother let me check out a Bible from the local library. I sat on our olive green sofa and read the Gospel of John from beginning to end in one sitting. I read about Jesus opening the eyes of the blind and raising the dead. He was beaten and whipped while people yelled, "Kill the King of the Jews." I wondered, "Who was the King of the Jews? Who are the Jews?"

I read it to the end, but I didn't understand that the ending was about Jesus. There was a disconnect, and I needed someone to explain it to me, but no one did. While I understood that there was a man who died, I didn't understand that it was Jesus who died.

It said that they put his body in a tomb. I didn't understand what a tomb was so I just disregarded it as unimportant. What I thought was that they put a dead man (I didn't understand that it was Jesus) on top of a rock, and three days later this man came back to life.

That brought me great joy because I had just started learning about death and dying. I knew that people died, and

I was terrified of death. After reading the Gospel, I thought that if you put anybody's body on a rock for three days they would come back to life.

I drew a picture of Jesus on the cross and showed it to my mother. "Your father is not going to like that," she said. I took and hid it.

Wanting to be like Jesus, I even imagined a blind boy coming to my classroom at Lincoln Elementary School. I visualized myself putting play dough on his eyes and telling him to go wash his eyes in the sink and that he would see.

Before I could really understand those stories, my parents divorced. Mom disappeared, and my father took us to his country where I lived three years. In his country, people were very ready to tell me about Jesus. They said He was a great prophet, but that there was another prophet who was greater, Mohammed.

Not knowing any better, I believed it. All I knew was that I was a Muslim—not a Christian. In fact, I hated Christianity because I thought Islam was the only truth and the only way to get to heaven. My world was so black and white. I was so spiritually hungry, and I became very devout.

In our madrassah we would learn from the imams, who would come and explain the Koran to us. They told us about heaven—*al jenna*—a place where you could ask for grapes or any food you wanted any time you wanted, and you would get it. We were too young to be told about the virgins. I was so religious, and my friends and peers knew it.

There was one girl in our village who was a Christian like her mother. People often talked about her behind her back because she dared to wear a cross necklace. Because she spoke good English, I always went to visit her at her job. Sometimes we would talk for hours. I used to tell her about Islam because I wanted her to become a Muslim.

One night, as I spoke to her, she told me how Jesus said, "The man who dips his hand with me will betray me." The Holy Spirit touched my heart, and I was shocked. I knew what she was saying was the truth.

"That's the truth!" I told her. "That's the truth. I am a Christian." I was so excited. I couldn't wait to tell my friends. That opportunity came quickly.

Later that night, I was watching television with a group of friends when a girl mockingly put on a cross necklace they had on another girl's neck. I said to the girls, "That's the truth. I'll tell you about it later."

The girl with the cross said, "No, the truth is in the Koran." Something else touched my heart. I went back to Islam.

After three years, my father brought me back to the U.S. I would go work with him. He would go to farmers markets and sell radios, clothes, and shoes every weekend. I hated going with him, but he made me go.

I would listen to music all the time. I listened to "Carry On My Wayward Son." The word *son* irked me and fascinated me. It made me think of Jesus. I shouldn't have thought about it so much, but I was intrigued by the idea of God having a Son. If He had a Son, I wondered if He would be like Jesus—so kind, forgiving, and powerful.

Still, my allegiance was to Islam. I drew pictures of AlBuraq, the horse that carried Mohammed to the Seventh Heaven from the mountain in Jerusalem. I wasn't allowed to draw Mohammed, though, so I would cover his face when I drew him. I had a Koran, and I read it as much as I could but had a hard time understanding it. I would often take the Koran, sit in my living room, open it, and pray that Allah would do a miracle in my life. I asked him to give me a sign that he loved me, but I was always left disappointed.

After I was in the U.S. three years, I started high school. There was a kid named Brad. He wasn't like all the others. He didn't try to be cool, take drugs, or drink. He was really clean-cut and friendly. One day, we cut class together and went to the library. I asked him if he had the album, *One of These Nights*, by the Eagles, because I wanted to borrow it. He didn't, but he kept trying to talk to me about Jesus.

"I'm a Muslim," I told him. "I don't believe the Bible."

He kept trying and failing. Finally, he said, "Okay, let's talk about the Eagles."

Even though I didn't accept his words, I think just hearing them did something to me. On my way home from school I became angry at Allah for never answering my prayers. I said, "Okay, Jesus, if you're up there, you answer my prayers."

I quickly retracted that prayer and repented to Allah for even considering it. But these little steps must have started something in my heart.

Not long after, one night in 1978, I was alone in my home. My father, as usual, was gone for the weekend. *Saturday Night Live* was over, and the only thing on TV was this Oral Roberts program about Easter. I'm not sure what he was talking about, but suddenly—whooooosh!—I felt the Spirit of God fall on me in awesome power.

I was lying down and looked up at the ceiling, and I knew Jesus was right there. I didn't see Him with my eyes, but I knew He was there. It was right near the same olive green sofa where I had read the Bible as a child. It was the same Jesus I had fallen in love with eight years earlier. I knew Him!

I also knew He was the Son of God. As a Muslim I would never say that, but I knew He was. I was so happy.

This is what I was looking for in Islam all those years—life! The life is in Him and only in Him. Jesus is the life! I felt like I had been dead, and I came to life. I was so excited and overjoyed. My heart was flying on the wings of heaven. I knew Jesus was in there with me.

There was no one else around to tell, and I wanted to tell someone. I wasn't wearing a shirt so I took the *Close Up* toothpaste in my bathroom, which is red in color, and painted a cross on my chest.

A few days later, I went to the church that I always used to spit on. I met a pastor named Gary. I told him what happened to me. He was excited and asked me, "Do you know the only sin that cannot be forgiven?"

"Murder?" I asked.

He said, "No. It's not receiving Jesus as your Savior. Every other sin God forgives."

I learned the four spiritual laws and accepted Jesus into my heart that night, even though I think I already had surrendered to Him.

I didn't tell my father what had happened to me, but my sister who was in the Old Country came to the U.S. a few months after I became a Christian. She was a devout Muslim at the time. She was very upset when I told her, and she told my dad. That night, when I came home from my friend's house my father and sister were sitting together on the sofa. My dad told me to sit down. He said, "Ali, we're a family, aren't we?"

"Of course, we're a family," I said.

"We're Arabs, aren't we?" he continued.

"Of course, we're Arabs, Dad," I said.

"Ali, we're Muslims, aren't we?" he asked. I remembered reading in the Bible I had taken from the church that if you deny Jesus in front of men that He will deny you before God.

I said, "No, Dad. I'm not a Muslim anymore."

"Why?" he asked.

"Because, I'm happy like this," I said.

My father threw a shoe at me and told me to leave the house. Before I reached the door, he grabbed me and started trying to talk me back into accepting Islam. My dad sat on one side of me and my sister on the other. They kept preaching to me for what seemed like forever. Finally, they stopped and I went to bed.

By that point, I had been attending two different churches. Somehow my father found out about those churches and went to them and said that if I returned he would sue them. Since I was only fifteen, both churches asked me to honor my father and not return.

The devil tried to destroy my life after this. I started drinking, taking drugs, and getting into illicit sexual relationships. I became very rebellious and was so empty and alone.

One night, I went to the theater and watched two movies: *Carrie* and *Magic*. Both were very dark and satanic. When I went home, I became terrified of the future. I was so scared that I didn't want to live. I had a bottle of sleeping pills with me. I took all of them, around fifteen, and then lay down to die on my bed.

All of a sudden, as I was lying down, I felt the Holy Spirit pulling Himself away from me. I hadn't been to church for so long, and I didn't know that God was even with me. When He started pulling Himself away from me, I knew that He had been with me all along.

I begged Him not to leave me. He stayed with me, and I cried and cried. The next day I went to the church that I first went to and told them that I needed to be with them. The youth pastor took a real interest in me and kept in touch with me.

Eventually, my father did kick me out of our home, and I went to live with my mother. She allowed me to go to church. As I grew in the Lord I began to realize that although I believed in the Bible and had had an amazing conversion experience, I was still thinking like a Muslim.

I failed so many times to live up to what I felt I should be as a Christian, and I always came under extremely heavy condemnation. I was also terrified that God would leave me because I was so unworthy.

On the night of Father's Day in 1984, I was watching "A Father's Day Special" with Barbara Walters on television. There were several celebrities who were speaking about their fathers and how their fathers were their heroes. As I watched, I started crying uncontrollably as I felt that my father wasn't my hero.

I couldn't stop the tears. And then the Holy Spirit came to me and whispered; "You can call me Dad now." I was shocked when I heard those words. Although I had heard that I had been adopted into the family of God as a believer, it had never sunk in until then.

I knew at that point that I had not changed my religion. I did not go from being a Muslim to being a Christian. Rather, I had been in the kingdom of Satan and was now adopted into the family of God. I had been dead and had come to life.

I realized that as a son I had privileges and rights as a member of the family. I had authority as a son of God. I had the right to come before my Father without fear.

For me the most important lesson I learned is that I didn't have to be afraid of God leaving me. I learned that the relationship between a Father and a son is much stronger than that between a servant and his master, which is the way I felt in Islam.

If a servant fails to keep his master's order, he is fired or rejected from his service. That's not the case with a son. A son is a permanent member of the family and household. That gave me a newfound confidence in my relationship with God.

After this revelation of my new identity as a son of God, the Holy Spirit led me to memorize Galatians 4:1-7 like this:

> *Now I say that an heir, as long as he is a child, differs nothing from a servant though he be lord of all, but is under tutors and governors until the time appointed of the father. Even so, [Ali], when he was a child, was in bondage under the elements of this world. But when the fullness of time had come, God sent forth His Son made of a woman, made under the Law to redeem [Ali], who was under the law, that [Ali] might receive the adoption of a son. And because [Ali] is a son, God has sent forth the Spirit of His Son into [Ali's] heart, crying, Abba, Father. Wherefore, [Ali] is no more a servant but a son, and if a son, then an heir of God through Christ.*

4

THE TESTIMONY OF JAMIL

I was stuck on this street corner in my uniform with my gun by my side. People came to regard us as terrorists, but most didn't even notice us.

When I started this particular phase of my life, two things gripped me: my need and my passion. My need was for stable work, while my passion was for freedom for my people and myself. These were the thoughts that filled our minds as youth and were nurtured with a barrage of media, social, and religious indoctrination.

Lighting my fourth cigarette, I was just standing guard at the intersection. Depending on who came to the checkpoint, I knew what to do. We had special training to deal with friends, enemies, average folks, and just about any other situation we would come up against.

But I was hardly ready for the passengers of a car who drove by and smiled at me. You don't know what it means when foreigners smile. Is there a trap? But for me, *that* day, a smile was so welcome. I really wanted someone to smile at me, and I really wanted to smile back.

Smiling back I think was more important than being smiled at. I needed to give something other than the rough visage that I was trained to display.

These smiling foreigners handed me a small, shiny, green booklet. I took it and thanked them. In decorated religious looking script it said, *John*, in Arabic, *Yohanna*. Who was John? I had read the Koran many times, and I didn't remember a John. This book looked like a teaching on the Koran. I was bored, and I started reading in between puffs. I was intrigued as I read: "In the beginning was the Word, and the Word was with God, and the Word was God."

"Who is this? What is this?" I asked myself. I looked around me in fear to make sure no one was watching me. Still, I couldn't put it down and had to read on. I lit another cigarette as my boredom turned to excitement.

"Through Him were all things made, and without Him nothing was made that had been made."

I thought, "What? What are these words? What are they saying? Why weren't we taught this?" I had learned about God all my life in school and in the mosque, but I had never learned about this before.

Then I read the words that stunned me: "The Word was made flesh and dwelt among us."

"Shouldn't I know this? Who is this?" I closed the book and looked at the cover and the back of it. I opened the front pages and looked for a picture or something to help me understand, but I only found these words. It felt like they were prying my eyelids open. The words were churning inside me like a torrent of questions that I didn't how to ask.

I put the book in the inside pocket of my green camouflaged vest. It was windy. I enjoyed the wind. I wanted to feel something familiar. It felt like I was drawn into a spiritual battle I couldn't retreat from. "Where would it lead me?" I thought. "Why did they give me this book? Why me?"

I looked around at the other people walking and talking with each other. They weren't conflicted like I now was. Their lives were so simple. Could my life go back to that kind of carefree simplicity I had known a few minutes ago? I would soon learn that the answer was *no*.

At night in my barracks I didn't talk to anyone. I smoked a cigarette and drank a small Turkish coffee. I felt around in my vest pocket and pulled out the book. If anyone asked I would tell them it was religious poetry. I read and read and read. I couldn't stop. This man who was doing these miracles mesmerized me. The exhaustion of the day finally caught up with me; as I put my head on my pillow to think about what I had read, I fell fast asleep.

As I lay in deep slumber, I felt warm water running down my face. I wiped it off, but when I looked at my hand it wasn't water—it was blood! Terrified, I lifted my head and looked up. I saw a man suffering on a cross. His blood was running down onto me. Somehow I knew that the blood ran down on me for a reason. What was the reason? I grabbed the wood of the cross and wept. What did this mean? I woke up confused. What was going on? I couldn't tell anyone, or they would think I was crazy or possessed by a devil, and that I was a Kafir or heretic.

I had to find out quickly. In the morning, I left the barracks and went to a city in the north where there were a few churches. When they saw my uniform, the people were afraid that I was trying to entrap them. They refused to talk to me.

I felt helpless. I told my sister and she was enraged. She told me I would have to stop this foolishness before I disgraced the family and maybe even got killed for talking about a man on a cross.

She was even more scared that I would be considered a Kafir. It would be the greatest shame for my family—a stain that would never be wiped away. My sister wasn't married yet. If people found out that I was a Kafir, no one would want to marry her because of the reproach and shame.

Still, I couldn't rest. I had to know the meaning of my dream and the little green book. I traveled to the northernmost city in my country. I knew there were Christians there. I didn't go to the church, because I was afraid they would reject me like the others had done. Instead, I went to a Christian bookstore where I met a man named Tarek.

Like the others, he looked at my uniform and seemed reluctant to talk to me. "To each man an answer," he said, as if he were talking to himself. We sat down, and he asked me to tell him everything.

I spoke so fast and erratically that I expected him to tell me to stop, but he just nodded his head in agreement as if he understood everything I was saying. It was such a relief to meet someone who understood.

When I was done, he opened the book, the Injil, and started pointing out the different aspects of my dream and the green book. He told me about Jesus. He was the One who made everything. He was the One Who was with God in the beginning. He was the One who was God! Then he told me that Jesus was also the One of whom it says, "He became flesh and dwelt among us...."

His words just sank in with such power and conviction. They flowed inside me like a cool river of quenching living waters. I was full of life and joy.

Tarek went on to explain the dream, the nails, the wood, the Man, and the blood. The man I dreamed about was the same Man of Whom it was said, "...all things were made by Him."

He was the same person of Whom it was said, "...the Word was with God and the Word was God." Why would God allow Himself to die in such agony?

Tarek said it was all because of love. God loved the world so much that He sent Jesus to die for it to save it. He didn't need to explain. I knew that everything he said was true. Still, there was one thing I still didn't understand. I asked, "Why was the blood on me?"

"Because the blood of the Crucified Man cleanses away all our sins," he said. "We are all sinners in need of forgiveness. The blood is the source of forgiveness."

He showed me the way of salvation. It was so in line with all I had been feeling and thinking over the last few days. It was like water to a thirsty man. I cried with tears of joy. Tarek said I was now a son of God. I surely couldn't understand this, but I accepted it and knew that God would teach me what it really meant.

I felt such great joy, but I was afraid for my family. They knew what had happened to me, and they were terrified for me. I called my sister and told her everything. She yelled at me and said I could never return to the house because I was a Kafir.

I asked Tarek to pray with me for my family and specifically my sister. We prayed together, and I felt as if God told me that everything would be alright. After a few weeks of wandering in the North, attending churches, and learning more and more about Jesus, I decided to try calling my family again. My sister answered. She was so different from before.

I didn't understand. She even apologized to me. She said that I could come to the house and that my parents were waiting for me. I went, and they welcomed me. I didn't think I could tell them everything because it was too much of a shock. They already knew what had happened to me, and they kept asking so many questions.

As I answered, they all became convinced. They all knew that I wasn't lying, and they accepted Jesus the same way I did. All but my six-year-old sister, Sabila, started going to Bible study with me and accepted the Lord Jesus.

One morning, as we were all eating breakfast she seemed to be smiling uncontrollably. When she saw that we were all looking at her she asked, "Do you notice anything different."

"No," we all said.

"Well, I accepted Jesus, too," she said.

5

THE TESTIMONY
OF BASSEM

After standing around in one place for too long, I used to get fidgety. Twenty-three years ago, when I had started working, I was hit in the head by a moving crane. I fell to the ground. It felt like someone was hitting my head over and over and over. A ringing sound in my ears turned to a gradually faster drumbeat that got louder and louder. Unable to stop the pain or the noise, I faded out. I woke up days later in a hospital. For months, I would fade in and out.

After that, my gait was a little stilted, and my right shoulder drooped. My head leaned to the right, and my left eye squinted even when there was no light. It didn't matter anymore, since I just lived day in and day out trying to make enough money to feed my kids. Most of the time I couldn't even find work. My brother, Maged, and I pooled our resources together, trying to make ends meet. He was getting tired of me, too, since I owed him so much money. I also owed money to my father and the grocery store.

I worked as a janitor at an apartment complex owned by one of the wealthiest families in the city. The owners were nice enough to employ me, but they barely paid me enough to buy food for my family.

I usually took the 120 dinars I got every month and bought a carton of tomatoes, cucumbers, and potatoes. Every few months, I got some sugar, salt, coffee, and tea as well. We very rarely could afford meat, although we sometimes managed to get some sardines.

Everyone began talking about this new couple who had moved down here to work with the Red Cross. The man's name was Robert, and his wife's name was Natalie. They were Christians.

We had only about ten Christian families in the whole town, and they stayed to themselves, while we did the same. I talked to Robert and Natalie a couple of times; they seemed really nice. She didn't speak very good Arabic, but he did. He would always invite me to their apartment on the fourth floor.

Because of the head injury I had suffered when I was younger, I sometimes lost my concentration and started drifting. One day I had a terrible headache that just wouldn't stop. I took aspirin and tried everything I knew, but it didn't work. Because of my injuries, my headaches often led to deep depression.

I was collecting the trash from the residents going up and down in the elevator when Robert was leaving for work. I told him about my headache.

Without even asking my permission, he put his hand out and said, "In Jesus Name, be healed."

About five seconds later, this dark cloud that had been over my head just lifted. There was no other way to describe it. It was as if a thick cloud of depression and pain just dissipated. My head felt better. My emotions were giddy. I started telling everyone what Robert did.

I stayed at the apartment complex until he got home that night. I put my hand on my head and said to him, "That thing you did. It worked. My head is better."

One of the owners of the complex came up and said to Robert, "Here, put your hand on my head. I'm sick of everything, too."

Robert seemed so encouraged, and he invited me up to his house; then we had tea together. When I went home, I kept tossing and turning in my sleep.

I had a dream. I saw a man in a white robe. He was about thirty years old, and he smiled so lovingly at me. He said, 'You are my son, and I am coming soon."

I thought, "Who was this man? I had never seen him before. Why was he smiling at me? Why did he call me his son? What did he mean when he said he's returning?"

The next day, when Robert got home from work, I went up to his house. He was watching a movie on his computer. I couldn't believe what I saw on the screen. It was the man in my dream.

"Who is that?" I demanded.

"That's Jesus, or as you call Him, Isa the Messiah," Robert said. "This movie is called *The Life of Jesus*."

I told Robert about my dream. Robert was ecstatic, and he explained to me who Jesus was and what he had done for us. I was overjoyed as I heard the words. I was so amazed that the same man in my dreams was the man in the movie. Robert told me that many Muslims had dreams about this man, just as I did. He said that Jesus had come to the earth and died for me. As a Muslim, I had been taught that Jesus didn't die on the cross. But when Robert spoke, something in my heart knew that what he was saying was true.

"Yes, this is the truth," I said.

He told me to pray a simple prayer. He told me word by word what to say. I felt like light had just driven all the darkness out of my broken body. The depression and pain were gone. I felt new. I was crying with joy. I hugged Robert and kissed his face. Robert told me that I should be careful about telling others, because many people might oppose me. I knew that already. I knew what happened to people who changed their religion. But, I couldn't deny the life I felt when I heard about this man Jesus.

I started going over to Robert's house as often as I could. I always made the sweet minty tea that Robert loved. We would sit and talk for hours about Jesus. He would have me read the Bible. When I read, I would feel a power surging through my body. Then one of Robert's neighbors named Hatem noticed our friendship and started hanging out with us.

Little by little, Hatem started asking questions, and he too prayed and asked Jesus to come into his life. We became three. We'd sit together and talk about Jesus and sing songs. Robert would play the keyboard and teach us Arabic Christian songs. When we sang together, I felt like I was in heaven.

One day, after Robert had gone to work, Hatem and I were standing outside the apartment complex. I really needed some money. I remembered one of the songs that Robert had taught us. It said, "I love you Jesus, help me live right. I love you Jesus, I'm Yours all the way."

I loved that song, so I sang it like this: "I love you Jesus, give me peace. I love you Jesus, give me joy. I love you Jesus, give me money." Hatem heard me, and we laughed together at the funny song. About fifteen minutes later, while we were still standing there, a man I didn't know came up to me, smiled, and shook my hand; then he gave me 50 denars. Hatem and I looked at each other in disbelief. What had just happened?

When Robert came home, I told him what had happened. I was sure he would be amazed. I said, "I've prayed to Allah for forty years and have never received anything. Why, when I prayed now, were my prayers answered?"

Robert said, "It's because now you have the key. The key is the Name of Jesus."

Hatem and I were always spending time with Robert. We were enjoying fellowship and learning about Jesus. We tried to be secretive, because if our neighbors knew about us it could be trouble for us.

I had another dream. It was a very strange dream. I told Robert about it the following day. In the dream, Robert was speaking to me. He said to me words I didn't understand in English: "Do as I do."

When I told Robert, he asked me, "Do you know what those words are?"

I said, "No."

He told me that the words were English, and he translated them into Arabic for me. Then he asked me, "Was there anything else in the dream."

And I told him, "Yes."

In the dream, I was doing the ceremonial cleansing that Muslims do before prayer. I was washing my hands and feet in the dream, and Robert said, "No, that's not the right way. Let me show you the right way." Then, Robert dunked me into a pool of water.

I told Robert the whole dream, and he was amazed. He said that the experience I had dreamed about was called "baptism." There were no pools of water nearby so Robert told me to bring a robe and come to his house the next day. He said he was going to baptize me in his bathtub.

I did as he said. I stood in the bathtub, and he poured water over my head. I started shaking and yelling, "I feel God. I feel God." It felt like I was a new man.

One day when we were studying the Bible, Robert taught me about tithing and giving money to the church. There were no churches where we were, but I felt so challenged to give. Even though I had barely enough money to buy food, I felt I had to give. Of the 100 dinars I had, I gave Robert fifty to give to the church.

He prayed for me that God would open the windows of heaven over my life. He told me how God promised to bless those who give. I went home feeling energized, even though I had so little money. Then a man I hadn't heard from in years called me and told me to go to his house. When I went, he opened up his basement and showed me a room full of women's purses. He said he had had them for years, and he didn't know what to do with them. He gave them to me, and I went and sold them at the bazaar. I made about 500 dinars. That same week, after months of being unemployed, I received three job offers. God indeed opened the windows of heaven and blessed me.

6

THE TESTIMONY OF Yacoub (Jacob)

All of us were trained in Islam from a young age. My siblings and I would never be allowed to stray from the mosque. Our family had produced some of the best known and most respected Muslim leaders in the country.

Our family name, Al Hussein, was synonymous with religious rigor. We were always called on to lead prayers. My brothers and I were often asked to do the call to prayer because of our strong voices. My grandfather never missed a prayer.

As I grew older, I knew that I would be called on to pursue religious training. Like many of my generation, I had a wandering eye. I wasn't able to just commit to the strict Islamic lifestyle that my family was trying to bequeath to me, but I played along. I believed, but I was open-minded too. In fact, my family, in spite of their deep commitment to Islam, was also very open-minded, or so I thought.

Mel was a teacher from Europe. He came to our country to help with the distribution of food and emergency supplies in our community. Something about him intrigued me, but I didn't know what it was. He was different from all the people I had known.

I spent a lot of time with him and asked him many questions. Because of my own changing attitudes, I was curious to know what westerners thought about Islam. Mel never spoke against Islam; instead, he just spoke about Jesus in a way I'd never heard before.

He spoke about Jesus as if He was his real friend. I wanted that kind of a relationship with God. Could God be a friend? In Islam, I was always so terrified of God, that He would judge us in the last day in such a terrifying manner. I had nightmares of the Day of Judgment when I would have to walk on a sword's edge over hell. If my good deeds outweighed my bad deeds, I'd make it across, but if not, I'd fall in and be tormented. To ensure our entry to *aljenna* (heaven), I was told I had to pray five times a day. I had to fast all of the month of Ramadan. I had to give money to the poor and say the creed: "There is no God but Allah, and Mohammed is his messenger." Then, at some point in my life, I was supposed to go to Mecca and walk around the Kaaba seven times and kiss the rock to get forgiveness of my sins.

Even if I did all these things, I could never be sure I would get to heaven. Some imams told me to just be good and love my neighbor. Some told me to pray more and fast more and give more. I went to Mecca and walked around the stone, but I didn't feel any better. All the people I've seen go to Mecca seem like they're better for a few days; and then they're back to the way they were.

Some of us younger men just went along with the traditions with which we grew up. Some were more religious than others. Many of them, like me, knew we'd never make it to heaven. We lied, we stole, and we gambled. The real bad ones even drank liquor, but in front of our families we avoided making waves. We just played along.

In our hearts, most of us knew we had no hope of making it to heaven. We were just biding our time until we had to walk on that dreadful sword or look at the *mizan* (scales) where our good works and evil works would be weighed.

If I ever asked anyone if they were sure they were going to heaven, they would answer, "*Inshallah*" or "God willing." No one ever knew for sure, which was so frustrating to me. I had seen my grandfather working so hard to do all that was required of him, and yet, I wasn't sure he would go to heaven.

Mel seemed to know for sure that he would go to heaven. I wanted to have that assurance, but I thought I knew myself too well to ever be sure I was going to heaven. I spent more and more time with Mel. I told him how I admired his faith though I didn't agree with him about his theology. One day, unexpectedly, he asked me if I wanted to have that same assurance of salvation like he had.

"No one could be sure," I told him. "It's up to God."

When he told me that we could be sure, it completely shocked me. He said that the only way to be sure is if I would enter on someone else's merit, not my own.

"Every man will be judged for his own sins and righteousness," I told him.

He continued to explain to me how, that if we base our eternal hope on our own good works, we could never be sure that we could go to heaven. I already knew that. I stopped arguing and just listened. He told me how Jesus was born to die to take my sins away. He died and suffered for my sins so I didn't have to. Although, that went against everything I had always been taught, I just listened because deep in my heart, I hoped it was true. It seemed so wild to me that someone would pay for my sins, but I took some comfort in knowing that Mel really believed it; therefore, it couldn't be that outlandish.

He continued to expound on the message of the Gospel to me little by little. I was stunned to hear that Christians actually believed that. As Muslims, we try so hard and work so hard to get God to approve of us, but Christians think that God approves of them because of Jesus' merit. How could that be?

He opened the Bible and asked me if I would read Isaiah 53. Even though I was open-minded, I was very uncomfortable holding a Bible. But I was curious.

I read it and was intrigued, but it was so difficult to understand. I asked if I could take the Bible and read it by myself. Mel agreed.

That night, as I was alone in my room, I took the Bible out of my case and opened it to the page I had read with Mel. I read it over and over again. Even though I didn't fully understand it, something happened inside of me as I read it. My mind opened up, and my heart softened: "...he was wounded for our transgressions, and by His stripes we are healed." Those words rolled over and over in my mind all night long; and in the morning I understood.

"Of course," I said. "It has to be this way. We could never be good enough."

I took the Bible back to Mel that day and told him what I learned. It was as if a light entered my heart. I wasn't ready to accept Jesus as my Savior, but I told him I wanted a Bible of my own. He gave me a small one and told me to read the Gospel of Luke.

I would stay up for hours each night reading it. It got to the point that I couldn't go a day without reading the Bible. I loved the stories of Jesus healing the sick and raising the dead. I had never known this kind of life in Islam, and I knew what I had to do.

The next night I went to see him again. "I think I'm ready now," I said. He prayed with me, and I received Jesus into my heart. What happened inside me was so strange. It felt like light came in and darkness left. I didn't feel any different, but I knew it was right.

I also knew what this would mean in my family, but I didn't expect it to happen so quickly and so severely. I stopped going to the mosque and stopped praying on Fridays. My family became suspicious, and my father especially noticed. I went home one night and found my Bible and tapes in a pile in the middle of the living room. My father was standing with my brothers.

"What's this?" he asked even though he knew. I didn't answer at first. "Is it yours, or did someone put it in your room?" my father continued.

All I could say was, "It's mine."

That was enough. My father grabbed me by my neck and slapped me mercilessly. He dragged me on the ground, and my youngest siblings started screaming while my mother cried.

"You're not my son!" he said. "Take everything and leave! Now!"

"Where is he going to go, now?" my mother implored. He looked at her, and she didn't speak again but kept crying. Finally, my father said that until I found a house, I could stay in the donkey's stable.

I cleaned a spot in the stable and moved my things out there. I read the Bible by the streetlight while streams of glory flowed through me.

I wanted to go to church so bad. Each time I did it seemed someone was following me, and there would be a major flare up at my home. I finally decided to just stay to myself. I also did my best to reconcile with my family without denying my faith.

I met another man name Husam. He was like me, a Muslim who became a Christian. He was very bold, and he seemed to understand what I was going through. I stayed with him for a while. He was very kind and patient with me. From the first time he met me, he told me he didn't want to call me by my Muslim name, Mohammed. Instead, he called me Jacob.

I was still limping from the beating, and Husam said I reminded him of Jacob in Bible. He told me he wrote a poem about me.

Jacob's limping down the street
He's been touched by something
Someone, human eyes can't see.

Jacob's on the run tonight
The darkness tried to make a stand
With violence of human hands.

Jacob was a wrestler too
With an angel in that darkness
The sinew broke the limping started.

No, he'll never walk the same
Because his heart forever changed
The world one day will come to see
What now behind the pain concealed.

But the glory that's inside
For a few days in this night
Seems to in the darkness hide
But one day it will shine so bright.

Jacob's limping down the street
He's been touched by something
Someone, human eyes can't see.

I went back home and just stayed to myself. I didn't talk about God or religion with anyone. I stopped going to church, and I tried to not make any waves with my family. This worked for several years, and then things became more and more convoluted. My father would go through seasons where he would pressure me and threaten to throw me out of the house. Other times, he would relent and take me back into the home.

One day, I grew so despondent about my situation. I looked at my life and felt hopeless. My brothers all had homes, wives, and children. They had jobs and were standing on their own two feet. I was unable to get work. I had no money or home.

In my distress, I decided to go back to Islam. I told my family that I saw the light, and that I was just naive before. They were overjoyed. They made a huge party for me. At the mosque, news of my return to Islam was greeted with elation. They asked me to make a video of myself describing my fall away from Islam, my entrance into Christianity, and then my return to Islam. It was to be called, "My return to the True Light."

Husam had been very concerned for me, and he stood by me through so many hard times. I didn't want to make this decision without telling him. He tried really hard to dissuade me, but I told him I had made up my mind.

"If you want, I will stop being your friend," I told him.

His head drooped in sadness and thought. "No, I will be your friend if you want," he said.

The weeks went on. I was still being celebrated by my family and the mosque. I was a hero, and they had big plans for me. They wanted me to describe for all Muslims the deceptiveness of Christianity and Christians. The emptiness I'd known before I met Jesus was creeping up on me. Even though everyone was being so nice to me, I knew it wouldn't last.

During this time a strange thing happened. I noticed that Jesus was still with me. Even when I went to pray in the mosque, Jesus was still there. He never left me alone.

It wasn't long before I was back at Husam's house. I told him that I wanted to come back to Jesus for good, no matter what it cost me. My family went through another upheaval. I was even arrested and beaten. The arm of the man who beat me broke a few days after he hit me. Another man, I'm not sure who, hit me with his car. I'm not sure it was related to my return to Christ, but it happened at the same time. When the car struck me, I fell on the ground and broke my nose.

I was back in the donkey shed. It was unbearable, but spiritually, things seemed to be improving a little for me. I started reading the Bible and being bolder in my witness.

My family knew about my relationship with Christ. While they haven't rejected Islam, my family seems to know that there is power in the Name of Jesus, and at times, they would ask me to pray for them.

One of my siblings had a very serious physical condition that doctors couldn't cure. I asked Husam to pray for him, and he was healed. Husam also had his friend pray for my sister when she was sick, and she was healed.

Other strange things happened as well. My grandfather, who was an Imam, got very sick and was taken to the hospital. He had tried many times to convince me to return to Islam. He had been frustrated with me, but when he got sick he called out for me. As he lay on his deathbed my family called me and told me to go stand with him. He didn't speak to me nor me to him. I just held his hand and prayed for him.

I had another uncle as well who was very old. As a last act, he was to say the creed: "There is no God, but Allah and Mohammed is his prophet." All the men from our family surrounded his bed to hear him say the creed. They waited and the old Imam, who was greatly respected in the mosque, said these words, "There is no God but Allah, and Jesus is His Son," then he died. Those words caused a huge uproar in the village, but they couldn't do anything because he had already died.

7

THE TESTIMONY
OF MAHMOUD

I know I am fortunate to have a job. So many of the young men in my village are unemployed. My job at the Zanzibar coffee house is very difficult. I have to leave my family for weeks on end. Sometimes, I don't see them for a whole month.

My wife gets very lonely, and my children miss me. The job situation is such that I have to take whatever I can. I usually come to work on the first or second of the month and go home for two days at the end of the month.

Usually, at night, after the customers have left, I sit at one of the tables in the outdoor courtyard and smoke. If a customer comes and orders anything, it's easy to go in and fix it for them. Very few people come by this late.

On one Wednesday night, two men came to drink coffee. They were both Arab even though one of them seemed like a foreigner. His Arabic was broken, but he spoke well and I understood him.

They told me they had just come from church. I told them that I was a Muslim, but that I loved Jesus. In fact, I had a picture of Jesus in my wallet that a Christian tourist had given me years earlier. I showed it to them. The name of the one with the broken Arabic was Jasser. He was really excited when he saw the picture of Jesus.

He told me that he too had been a Muslim, but that he was now a Christian.

"What happened to you?" I asked him.

He said that when he was a teenager; he was a very devout Muslim. He read the Koran and knew all the stories. He even tried to convert Christians to become Muslims like him. One night, he said he was listening to a program on the radio about Jesus. The preacher was talking about how Jesus died and came back to life on the third day.

"As the man spoke, the Spirit of God just fell on me," Jasser said. "I knew Jesus was in the room, and He filled my heart with so much joy and peace that it was indescribable. It was so powerful I could hardly move, but I knew then that Jesus is the Son of God."

As Jasser spoke, I couldn't help but love what he was saying. There really was something to his words, but I didn't know what it was, and I was a little scared.

"Do you want to accept Jesus into your heart?" he asked me.

I said, "No." I wasn't ready. I didn't know if I would ever be ready, to be honest, but I didn't want to tell him so. He seemed disappointed, but he was very nice to me. We talked for a long time, and then they left.

The next day, my brother Ahmed and I were walking in the city when we found Jasser sitting alone drinking coffee. We sat with him and talked for a long time. I told him that my brother was looking for a job but hadn't been able to find work.

Jasser asked if he could pray for my brother to find work. Even though my brother is a more devout Muslim than me, he didn't mind. Jasser prayed, "Father, in the Name of Jesus the Messiah, please help Ahmed to find work so he can meet his needs and plan for his future. You care about the birds--how much more do you care about us. Please help Ahmed."

Ahmed and I got up and shook hands with Jasser and left. About ten minutes after we left, we stepped into a small shop and asked if there was any work, and there was! After months of looking, we found work just as Jasser had prayed.

We finished all the paperwork and the job application, then we went back to look for Jasser, but he was gone. A few nights later, I went home for my monthly visit. I was so exhausted from the work and being away from my family. After the weekend, I got ready to go back to work, but I found out that I had been replaced at my job by the owner's nephew.

I begged him to take me back because I couldn't find work anywhere, but he wouldn't accept me back. I became despondent and lost all hope. I didn't even think of leaving the village because it was too expensive to go to the main city to find work. I wasn't sure what to do. I had two young children, and my wife was pregnant. I was trying to establish myself in the community, but you can't do that without a consistent source of income. I just had to keep borrowing money from my family. They were becoming angry with me, and I felt so guilty. I would go to the big cities once or twice a week to look for work, but there was nothing.

One night, my wife and I got into a bad fight. She kept telling me I had to find work and provide for the family. She was crying; I was yelling. The children were crying, and I felt so bad. I sat alone in the kitchen drinking coffee and smoking. I became despondent. I couldn't see any hope for the future. My wife was angry. My parents were angry. My children were growing, and I had no way to provide for them.

As I sat there, almost in tears, I saw a bright light in the window. It turned the whole room white. I was almost blinded by the brightness. Then, I felt this immense joy and peace that I had never felt before. I looked up and all around. I stood up. And then, I knew that Jesus was in the kitchen with me.

I sat back down. Was it real? It was. It is. The reality of His presence was so clear. I sat back down with tears of joy running down my face. I was overjoyed. He didn't say anything to me, but I know He was there. I felt like a new man inside. I had hope for the future. I didn't know where I would work or how, but I knew that He was with me.

I remembered Jasser and the story he told me of how he came to believe in Jesus. I hadn't talked to him since. It had been about seven months.

Around 2 p.m. the next day, I called him. He was still at work, but I couldn't wait to tell him.

"Jasser," I said.

"Mahmoud?" he said excitedly.

"Yes, this is Mahmoud," I said. "The One who came to you came to me!"

He didn't seem to believe me, so he changed the subject. He asked about my family and my work situation. We talked for about five minutes about where I had been and what I had been doing. Then, I couldn't contain myself any more, and I repeated myself, "Jasser!"

"What?" he asked.

"Did you hear me?" I said. "The One who came to you, came to me." This time, he didn't try to change the subject.

"Jesus?" he asked.

"Yes, Jesus," I said. "Jesus came to me last night."

I told him how I had been sitting in the kitchen and how I saw the light and felt the presence of Jesus. He was overjoyed and said we needed to get together. I told him I didn't have means to get to the city so he came to my village instead. We spent hours together talking about Jesus and what happened to me. He explained to me how Jesus had died for me. We prayed together. I knew I had found the Truth. I would also go to his house in the city and spend the night there sometimes. We would spend time with other Christians. I told him I had a hard time going to church because I wasn't used to girls without head coverings. I know it was something I had to overcome, but it made church attendance a real problem for me.

I did go to some night-time Bible studies. I loved the atmosphere of love between everybody. I also loved the teachings about Jesus and the music.

The first night I went I heard a worship song that says in Arabic: "I love you Lord Jesus. And there is none other. I will follow You always, Jesus. I will follow You without turning back. And I worship Your Holy Name and there is none other."

All night long, the song ran through my mind. It reached something so deep in my heart and pulled it out to the surface. It spoke exactly what I felt in my spirit and my soul. Worship music would become a big part of my life and relationship with the Lord.

I still had many problems, and the political situation in my country was very unstable so that it was very hard economically and socially. I still hadn't found a job and my family started complaining again. One night, as I was feeling depressed, I tried to sleep but wasn't able to get more than a few winks.

When the exhaustion finally got the best of me, and I didn't have the energy to worry anymore, slumber descended on me like a warm blanket. Then, I'm not sure if I was awake or dreaming, but I saw Jesus. He was standing next to my bed looking down on me. I looked up and saw Him. He put his hand on my shoulder and said to me, "Be patient and don't be afraid."

I could hardly wait to tell Jasser. He came over again and spent a few days in our village. Eventually, I got my old job back, and I was able to start providing for my family. Jasser, who lived in another city near the border, would come visit me once a month or so.

8

THE TESTIMONY OF ZAKI

My father was like a wall of protection around my siblings and me. He worked so hard to meet all our needs. And unlike so many Arab fathers, he also was very present for us emotionally. He didn't neglect us in anyway. If he suspected we were having any kind of problem, he would press upon us to divulge it and not to hide it from him.

He also protected us from much of the hatred that was aimed at the West in our culture. At our school and at the mosque, on the street and in the media, hatred of the West was the norm. It was the West that brought indignities upon my Muslim brothers and sisters. It was the West that was controlling the governments of the Arab and Muslim world. It was the West that sought to corrupt our youth with their technology and media.

Our whole society was indoctrinated in a strong resentment of the West. My father didn't seem to share that view like so many others. He seemed to find something to appreciate in the contributions of the western world. He liked their television channels. He liked the conveniences of modern life. He liked the ease of communications and transportation that the West afforded.

We were Muslims and faithfully attended prayer, but Dad just didn't allow our hearts to become receptacles of the hatred that we saw all around us. I was an average student. I always dressed well even when our family finances were tight.

My mother always made do with what we had. We never knew hunger. Our parents sheltered us from the truly devastating reality we lived in.

Religion, of course, was central to our community. Attendance at Friday prayers at the mosque was expected. My six brothers and I were always at Friday prayers with my father.

I always admired my older brother, Hamed. He took seriously his role as the oldest brother in our family. In our culture, the oldest male has to be ready to assume responsibility for the family in case anything happens to the father. He's the one who would help with its financial and social needs. Thankfully, he never needed to assume that role since my father, except for some mild arthritis, always was able to provide for us.

Hamed did, however, lead the way for the rest of his younger siblings in terms of marriage, child rearing, and establishing himself in the community. He laid down footprints that we could follow.

Hamed's kindness was reflected in his love for those less fortunate. I believe that was inherited from my father's kind heart and my mother's tenacious carefulness over us. Whereas so many of the young men from the Sultanate sought prestige, wealth, and reputation, Hamed sought to help the blind.

He loved the blind. He learned Braille and turned around and taught the blind how to read Braille. He started a house for the blind where he could help them learn, find work, and most of all be able to function in our society. It was very challenging, but I so admired Hamed, and I started helping him.

Soon, I found that I was spending all my time with the blind. I too, learned Braille and taught others. The excitement about what we were embarking on was contagious. Many in the community lauded our efforts with the blind, and many sought to help us by providing tools for our house for the blind.

During the early days of the *House of the Blind*, I was also attending occupational training classes in the capital city, which was about twelve miles east of our village. I would go there day after day and come home at night to the smell of my mother's cooking and the warmth and camaraderie around my father's table. We'd sit on mattresses on the ground around the table and discuss every minute detail of our days. Father wanted to know everything.

I especially loved, describing to my brothers and father, how I was mastering my new language skills. I was learning English and was exhilarated by the teachers who were all foreigners. One was Korean; we called her Chansey. None of us pronounced her name right, and she'd laugh along with us as we stumbled along learning English. There was one teacher that really inspired me. His name was Trevor. He was from England but was also an Arab. He knew Arabic and English perfectly. I also noticed that he wore a wooden cross around his neck.

In our community, there were very few Christians. We knew of some and heard about them, but we had very conflicted feelings about them.

On the one hand, we admired them. They were usually wealthier than the others in our community. They were also extremely kind. They were practically indistinguishable from the Muslims in many ways. They were proud of their Arab identity. They attended our schools, grew up with us, and played with us.

I often wondered why there seemed to be such a huge chasm between them and us. I supposed the same way my father found value in the West, in spite of the anti-westernism in our culture; I found something of value in the Christians.

They didn't seem to have the fear and guilt that we struggled with and tried so helplessly to overcome. What was it about them? One day, Trevor told me that he was going to have a special meal at his house.

He asked if I would like to come. I did. I wasn't at all nervous about going to his house. He had several guests, students, and staff from the school. We chatted and tried to practice our new English words that we had learned. I was completely captivated in the atmosphere of friendship and love I felt there.

There was something going on inside of me, but I didn't know what it was. I couldn't stay away from the *English Club* and especially from Trevor. We never talked about religion even though I saw his cross. He just seemed to understand me, and he seemed like he knew the struggle I was going through.

One day, I asked him to lunch. He agreed. I had a million questions I wanted to ask about Jesus, the cross, and the Bible. What did he think of Muslims, the Koran, and Mohammed? Did he know that Muslims revere the Bible and Jesus? Did he know that Muslims regard *Isa* (Jesus) as the Messiah and one of the greatest prophets?

He did. Trevor knew all about the Koran. Everything I told him, he understood. That shocked me. Why would someone who knows all this about Islam wear a cross around his neck? I didn't want to say anything, but wearing a cross was offensive to many people in the community. It almost always turned heads in the market place. Afterwards, whispers and suspicious glances would start.

What shocked me further was that Trevor also knew this. He seemed quite aware of the reactions his cross was having on the people around him.

"How do you feel about me wearing a cross?" he asked me one day.

"I don't have any feelings about it," I said. "But you know a lot of people are talking about you."

I so admired Trevor. He didn't seem to have a care. It wasn't because he was naive. It just didn't matter to him. That intrigued me and irritated me at the same time. In spite of this, I felt safe around him, and I felt safe to tell him: "A lot of people are talking about you. They say your father is a Muslim, and you're a *Kafir* (heretic). They say that's why you wear a cross."

I expected Trevor to tremble, but he didn't. He just looked at me and asked again, "Well, how does that make you feel?"

I had to be honest. Although I was trained in my culture to hate Christianity, I didn't. I loved Christians. I loved Trevor. I loved the way they were; and secretly, I wanted to have the same lightness and carefree spirituality that I saw in them.

"It doesn't bother me," I said. "I don't mind you wearing the cross. I just am concerned for you."

But it did bother me. Was he a *Kafir*? The Koran says of those who change their religion from Islam: "If they forsake you pursue them and kill them wherever you find them."

I didn't want to believe that. I stayed with the more moderate version of Islam that focused on verses like, "Your religion is your religion and mine is my religion." The Koran includes both verses, but some people believed that the more moderate verse had been abrogated, or replaced, by the more radical one.

Our discussion about the cross opened up a whole bunch of other questions in my mind. Had he been a Muslim? Why would he change? If he did change, why would he come back to this Muslim country where he could be hurt or even killed for rejecting Islam? I didn't ask these questions. The answers might force me to cut off this relationship that I truly enjoyed.

As our friendship grew, I started telling him about our house for the blind. We really wanted to launch it, and desperately needed help. Being from Europe, he could really help us. I started dropping hints about him coming to the house to meet the blind people. He always said he couldn't because of his work in the capital. I grew frustrated and eventually stopped asking.

Then, one night, as I was preparing for a meeting with the blind, I got a call, "Hey, Zaki. I'm here in your village. I came here for my job so I'd like to come see your house for the blind."

It was Trevor. I was ecstatic. I told some of the members of the *House of the Blind* to stay late and meet him. He came over and seemed intrigued by the building and the very few accessories we had. Then, he started talking with the blind. They loved him, and he seemed to genuinely love them. Little by little, he started developing a meaningful relationship with the *house*.

He seemed able to communicate and understand the limitations and needs of the blind. What happened next was shocking to me. Trevor called me and said he wanted to have dinner. We went out together, and he said he had something important to tell me.

He said he had lost his cell phone and had bought a new one. His new phone number was: 355-4216. "I kept trying to remember that number 4216, but I couldn't," Trevor said. "Every time someone asked me the number, I would give him the wrong number like 4126 or 6142."

Finally, Trevor said he decided to look in the Bible for help. He looked up Isaiah 42:16 and he was shocked. It said: "I will lead the blind by a way they know not."

As Trevor told me this, my knees started shaking. But there was more. He said he had told a friend of his in Britain about the verse in Isaiah. His friend from Britain told him to look up the first part of his phone number 355, or Isaiah 35:5. It says: "The eyes of the blind shall be opened!"

When he said that, I couldn't control myself. My whole body started shaking. I told him I wanted this religion. Trevor led me in a simple prayer: "Jesus, I believe you died for me on the cross and that you loved me. Come and live in my heart. Forgive me for my sins. I will follow you every day for the rest of my life."

I felt like I was a new person. I could not control the joy and the tears, even in the restaurant. Trevor was very reassuring. He went with me and spent the night at my home.

I can't describe the amazing joy that I started feeling as I started learning about the Bible and how to know God personally. I felt so light hearted and happy all the time. When I heard Christian songs, I felt I could soar to heaven. I also felt a responsibility to tell the blind about what I had discovered. I didn't tell them all, but I spoke to about five or six of them one by one. I told them to come with me to Trevor's house. They all seemed excited about what I told them.

Trevor was surprised when I showed up at his house with all the guys, but we sat and enjoyed some tea and coffee together. Then, to the business at hand: I asked Trevor to tell the blind what he told me the night before. He did. All of them instantly accepted the Lord!

Then Trevor did something I didn't expect. He told the blind that the Bible says that the eyes of the blind would be opened. He asked them if he could pray for their eyes to be opened. They all said "yes". Then he put oil on their eyes and prayed for each one. Nothing happened.

About a week later, one of the young men, Rami, was in his house when he started seeing light shining through his left eye. Slowly, things began to take shape, and he started seeing colors. He rushed to the house and told the others, and there was an electrical surge that seemed to flow through the house. Trevor came over and did some simple tests to verify if Rami was seeing, and he was!

It was incredible. But some of the members of our House who weren't believers began to grow suspicious and angry. They knew that Trevor was a Christian, and they knew that these miraculous signs were being done in the name of the Christian God, but the wonders continued.

One night, Trevor came over, and I felt my heart pounding inside of me so strong that I feared it would jump out of my chest. I took Trevor to the *House of the Blind* office and told him to pray for me.

"What do you want me to pray for you?" he asked.

"I don't know just pray," I begged him.

He put his hand on my head and started praying for me in a strange language, then all of the sudden the Holy Spirit flooded into me like a massive torrent, and I started shaking so violently I almost fell on the ground. Then my tongue just started speaking this new language all by itself. I didn't know what I was saying, but I felt electrified.

I had some of the blind come into the office, and I told them what happened. They asked me to pray for them. I put my hands on them, and some of them felt the presence of the Holy Spirit so strong they started shaking as well.

Several months later, Trevor asked us to go with him to a meeting at a church. There was a special celebration meeting because of Christmas. Trevor was acting in a play about the birth of Jesus. My brother Hamed and I went, and we took some of our friends who were not blind, and we took some of the blind as well.

Our friends, who are Muslims didn't complain, but they weren't too excited about going into a church. Because Trevor had helped us so much in our work with the blind, they decided to stay. After the meeting, we went to Trevor's house and decided to spend the night. Trevor's house was big enough to accommodate all of us. We slept on the sofas, on the floor, and on mattresses.

All of us were stunned by what happened the next day. After breakfast, we went back to our village. When we got back to the *House of the Blind*, Jilal, who is not blind, asked all of us, "Which one of you came to me last night? You were standing by my mattress and wearing a white gown. You stretched out your hand and said, 'I am the Christ and I am waiting for you.' Which one of you did that?" he asked.

We were all troubled. My brother Hamed was not a believer even though he had seen some of the miracles that had happened. I didn't know what to do. I called Trevor. Even Trevor didn't know what to do, but he told Jilal that he had to accept Jesus who had appeared to him, but Jilal was scared and refused.

News of the miracles got out. Some of the leaders from the mosque started sending representatives to our meetings to find out what was happening. One Friday, during our weekly meeting, members of the mosque came over and demanded of the blind who were present, "Who here likes the Christians?" Some of them who had been so helped by Trevor and other Christians he worked with raised their hands. The men started beating them. They even started breaking the furniture at the *house*. I was gashed on the side of my face.

We were all terrified, but we stood our ground. As soon as the men left, I called Trevor and told him what happened. Trevor told me to bring the blind and come to the capital city. We all got in a taxi and went. There were six of us.

When we got to the capital, Trevor met us and took us all out to one of the nicest restaurants in the city. We were all starving after our ordeal. He then took us to one of the nicest hotels and got rooms for all of us. We had never slept in hotels before. It was so luxurious and different to us.

Then Trevor put on a movie called, *The Passion of the Christ*. The blind heard the words and the dialogue, and they heard the noises of the beatings and screams of pain.

One of the blind, said: "That's what happened to us today."

Trevor looked at me. He was crying. I showed him the cut on the side of my face from the chair that hit me. I said to him, "What happened to me today doesn't compare with what happened to Jesus. I hope this scratch stays forever so I can remember that I was allowed to suffer with Him."

As our relationship grew, I spent more and more time with Trevor and his friends. I didn't want anything more than to know Jesus more and to grow in my love for Him. He was alive in me, and He was always with me no matter where I went.

One day, Trevor and I decided to invite some of the kids in the neighborhood who were very poor to go swimming at a nearby lake. We rented a big van and made it an all-day activity for the children. We ate lunch together, and then they went swimming.

I was wearing a suit jacket, my nice jeans, and shoes so I wasn't swimming, but Trevor was swimming with the kids and being a life guard too.

All of a sudden I felt inside me this strong urge to get baptized. I had talked to Trevor about it, but we never were able to work out the right time. Finally, I couldn't contain the longing any more. I just walked into the water wearing my jacket, jeans, and shoes.

Trevor asked me, "Are you crazy? What are you doing?"

I told him, "I want to be baptized."

Trevor said, "There are 300 Muslims here watching us, and you want to be baptized here?"

Finally, Trevor came up with a plan. He said, "Okay, let's pretend we're wrestling. You push me in the water; and then, I'll get up and push you in the water."

I pushed Trevor down, and he got up and grabbed me and pushed me under the water. "In the Name of the Father, Son and Holy Ghost," he said.

Then he pulled me up out of the water. I felt like a new man. As I walked back to the shore in a daze of joy and peace, I slipped on a rock and fell. My hand was gashed open by a cut that later needed twelve stitches.

Trevor was so upset. I told him, "Don't be mad. I feel like the water cleansed me and the blood purified me."

9

THE TESTIMONY
OF SAMEER

My Uncle Saeed was about eighty-years old now. He was dressed in the traditional oriental gown and head dress. He was the oldest member of our clan and therefore highly venerated.

I have known him since my childhood when I moved here to our village near the Holy City and the Blue Mosque. When I lived here, my father had to go back to America to work so Uncle Saeed became like a father to me.

He often took me to the Blue Mosque to pray, and he also took a great interest in my spiritual education. He was the first *Haj* (pilgrim) in our family, and he wanted all of us to be observant Muslims.

I remember when he came back from Mecca with his wife, Amti. They brought us all sorts of presents from Mecca. He bought me a small, green-plastic, television view- finder that had different sights from Saudi Arabia including: the Kaaba, Jabal Arafat, Medina, etc.

I went back to America after three years here, and I fell out of touch with Uncle Saeed and his family. But now, at thirty-years old, I was blessed to come on a tour of the Ancient Christian Churches in our country. I told the people on my ministry team that I had to break away from them one day to go see Uncle Saeed and my village. I asked them to pray for me because many people in my village knew that I had become a Christian. Many of them knew me when I was a boy, and they remembered how religious I was and how committed to Islam I had been.

I had a divine encounter with Jesus in the U.S. He changed my life, and I was now a pastor. This angered many in my village, and I didn't know how they would respond to my presence.

I knew that the Koran said that those who leave Islam are to be killed. What I didn't know was how far someone in my village would go to fulfil this mandate if they saw me.

My team members prayed for me. Some asked me not to come, but I felt I had to see Uncle Saeed because he was so old, and I hadn't seen him in over twenty years.

When I came to his house, I knocked and Uncle Saeed opened the door. He was frail. My heart ached at the sight of him. He looked at me through squinting eyes, not sure who I was.

"I'm Sameer," I told him. "Sameer, the son of Asa."

His eye brightened, and he invited me. His wife, Amti came out. She too was so frail. Her diabetes had eaten away at her muscle tissue. She could hardly walk, but she stood in the hallway telling me all about her grandchildren in America.

Since I live in America, I rarely have chances to see these family members. I didn't know how they felt about me, but I told them I was there on a work trip and that I could only stay for the afternoon.

We ate together and I ventured out on foot to some of my other relatives' homes. They were all cordial, but one Aunt looked at me and wouldn't smile. I could see the anger in her eye. She knew.

"Does your father know you're here," she asked.

I told her he didn't because it was such a short trip, but no one else even mentioned anything about my Christianity.

I returned to Uncle Saeed's house to say goodbye to him before leaving to go to the Old City. He came out alone to the gate where the taxi stood waiting for me.

We stood together in that sweltering heat as I prepared to return to the capital city. He was always so strong and controlled. He always had an answer. On issues of religion, he was the go-to man in our family. As the oldest member of our clan, he was the patriarch.

He knew that I had become a Christian, which was a great source of shame to my family. Most of the family wouldn't talk to me. Later on, some would even try to harm me.

Uncle Saeed didn't seem too concerned about all that right now. As I kissed him to leave, he let out a moan like I'd never heard before. I'd never seen him like this. His tears ran out like water fountains. I stood there trying to console him, realizing that I wasn't the reason for those tears. But I had touched something by my mere presence that triggered those tears.

I understood something, then, that changed my view of Muslims. As an ex-Muslim myself, I have firsthand knowledge of the subject, but I see so much in the media that can distort our picture of Muslims.

What I understood, then, is that Muslims are first-and-foremost human beings. They must be dealt with on that level. Jesus dealt with all people that way. In His encounter with the woman at the well in Samaria, He dealt with the most basic of human issues: thirst. She was the one who made an issue of the His race.

His disciples were the ones who made an issue of her gender, but He dealt with her only as a human being. In this way, He touched something in her that still touches all of us today. We need to have His heart first; then we can be His hands and feet, and then we can be His mouthpiece.

God loves the Muslims so much that He sent His Son to die for them. When they look at us, do they understand this?

I suppose the greatest ideal of a Christian is to be invisible so that people can see through us to Him. That's not realistic or the way that God wants it. He made us in His image to be who we are. He wants who we are to be like who He is. He told us to love our enemies because God loves His enemies. We were all God's enemies at one time. What did He do? He loved us and gave Himself for us.

When Hagar was cast out into the desert with her son Ishmael, the angel of the Lord met her and promised to bless the boy. He said that the boy would be a great nation. Islam, I believe, was birthed out of the rejection that Ishmael felt when he was cast out of his home. Rather than acknowledge his rejection, it was easier to say, as Islam says, that God has now rejected Isaac and has chosen Ishmael and his descendents instead. But in doing so, Islam has forfeited the great gift that God wanted to give to Ishmael and his descendents through Isaac. That gift is new life through the death and resurrection of His Son, Jesus the Messiah.

I experienced that life when He came to me in a supernatural way, perhaps similar to the way He came to Hagar. I knew He was Jesus, the Son of God, and I knew that He had died for me.

This seems to be the way God deals with Muslims all around the world. It's almost as if God has taken the initiative where the church has failed. Millions of Muslims come to Jesus every year. So many have the testimony of a vision or dream or miracle. They see a Man in a white robe who appears to them.

With God doing so much to reach the Muslims, we too, need to do much to reach our precious Muslim neighbors and friends. Although it's important, our focus is not to talk about Islam. Many of them know so little about Islam. It's to talk about Jesus.

When I was a young Muslim, I remember one of my aunts who had become a Christian. There was something inside her that moved her. She didn't preach to me, but her life touched me and made me want what she had. I now know; she had the Holy Spirit. That's what I wanted.

Our responsibility to the Muslim is no different than our responsibility to any other human. God doesn't see Bhuddists, Hindus, Christians, Muslims, Sikhs, atheists, etc. He sees people that He created in His own image that He sent His Son to die for.

Lord, give me Your heart,
To love like You do.

Lord, give me Your eyes,
That I might see through.

Lord, make me Your hands
That you can flow through.

Lord, make me Your feet
To come and go through.

10

THE TESTIMONY OF RAED

My mind was filled with wild thoughts. I had always heard that a Muslim who becomes a Christian will be cut to pieces.

Someone had seen me talking with Christians and reported me to the authorities. Two men came to me and said they wanted to get me a job, but it was a trap. They were secret police, and they had heard that I had become a Christian.

The two men picked me up and put me in the middle of the back seat of their car, with one man on my right and the other on my left. The driver didn't talk. The sun was so hot, and the silence in the car made it all the more terrifying.

"Will they kill me?" I wondered. My knees were shaking uncontrollably. All my life I had been required to attend Friday prayers at the mosque, where I heard what happens to Muslims who change their religion. The preacher's voice would always reach its highest decibels and pitch when he warned us, "They will be cut to pieces."

I was sure these men were going to cut me to pieces, and I tried not to think about it. But each time a pleasant thought crept into my mind, it was quickly beat back by the reality I was facing. "They might kill me," I thought. "How will they do it? Are there others waiting there too? Will they burn me with fire?"

"Jesus," I prayed in my mind. "Jesus, I heard so much of how You are able to protect me and keep me. I am so scared right now. I know that You are with me. Please help me. If I'm going to die, make me strong to not deny Your Name."

After what seemed like hours, the car stopped in front of a grove of trees. I was comforted by the sight of the trees because they seemed so beautiful compared to the ugliness I felt around me. The orange and yellow fruit looked so good, and I so badly wanted to stand outside for a while and eat one. But the two men grabbed my arms and escorted me into a room, an ugly dark room with ugly plastic, purple chairs. Everything was so ugly and depressing.

They signalled for me to sit down, and I did. My knees were still shaking, but for some reason, I was less fearful now. In the car, my imagination had been terrifying me with all the possibilities of what might happen.

Now, in this ugly, gray room, with these two dangerous-looking men, I didn't have to imagine what might happen anymore. Whatever was going to happen was going to happen.

I couldn't escape, so I didn't need to plan one. I couldn't call anyone to help, so I didn't need to think of what I would say. I just sat there.

"We hear that you like the Christians,"one man said.

"Yes, I do," I said with a boldness I didn't expect to have. "The Koran says that if we have questions, we should ask questions of the People of the Book. Christians are People of the Book."

"But, we hear that you are a Christian," he went on. "We hear that you are a Kafir, a heretic."

"Who told you that?"

"People told us," the second man said. He wasn't as threatening as the first. It was easier to look at him when I talked, so I did. As their questions continued, I found these men to be much less threatening than I had expected. There were no other people in the office either.

They seemed rather simple, to be honest. They didn't force me to say I was a Christian or a Muslim. We talked and talked; after a while, it seemed their main concern was that they didn't want to hurt me. They just wanted to scare me a little.

I felt ready to answer anything they might ask, even if it cost me my life. After a while, we got back in the car and headed back to the town square, where they had picked me up. I got out of the car. They didn't tell me good-bye or anything. I think they felt bad that they didn't rough me up or scare me more.

I don't know why they didn't hurt me, but I thanked Jesus so much that I was able to walk to my home. I hated my home and my town; but after this ordeal, my room felt like heaven.

From the tiny window in my room, I can see and hear the main market square. The outdoor bazaar is always loud with the sounds of taxis, trucks, and buses. There are also the many donkey carts that are wheeled in every morning as the farmers from the neighboring villages come to sell their produce.

My family is poor. I am one of six children. As the youngest boy, I was spoiled in my youth; but as I grew older, I learned that our world is cruel and hard.

It is almost impossible to find work. Unless you know the right people, it's hard to get ahead in our community. Our village is small, and everyone knows each other. If someone says something bad about you, it's almost impossible to overcome the bad reputation.

Like everyone in my village, my family is Muslim. We always went to mosque and learned the Koran. To tell the truth, I was always bothered by the fact that in the mosque they told us we are never to lie; if we lie, we will be punished by Allah. Once we got outside the mosque, those very same people would start lying and cheating just like before.

As a child, I always wondered how it could be like this. After a while, I just became hard like a rock. It was like I didn't even have a heart. I just accepted things as they are. People are like devils sometimes. They speak about each other behind their backs. They lie and steal, and then they always act religious in the mosque.

A strange incident happened when I was a teenager. A Christian woman came and stayed at my family's house for a few days. She saw how poor and miserable my family was, and she felt I would have more opportunities if I went and stayed in her city with her family. She said there were better schools and colleges there.

My family balked at the suggestion of me living with a Christian family. It was seen as the highest act of heresy to let their son live with Christians and be indoctrinated by them. Their answer was an absolute no.

My hopes were so raised by the prospect of leaving the sadness and poverty I knew. My mind was filled with thoughts of the city and the new school. I wanted so badly to be part of that new community with new people, but it wasn't to be.

I got so depressed that I could hardly concentrate on my school work. I was always a good student, but my emotions got the best of me. I didn't see any way out. I studied and worked to better myself, but it seemed like I just kept getting pushed back down. It was as if I was trapped in this miserable life and emptiness.

I couldn't stop thinking about Christian woman's offer. I was intrigued by the fact that she wanted to help me. I thought a lot about Christianity. Why were these Christians so nice to me?

In school and in the mosque, we were taught that Christians are sinners and blasphemers. They believe in three gods, and they are unclean because they eat pork and drink alcohol. She was nothing like this. I wanted to know more.

One day, I heard about a library that had Christian books in it. It was in a nearby city, and I could hardly wait to go there. I went and met a man who told me about the books they had.

His name was Jamal. I noticed that he was so bold in talking about the books. He said that they were about God and that God loved everyone so much. I had never heard that God loved me. I wanted to know more and more.

It seemed that for each question I asked, Jamal had an answer from the Bible. It felt like the answers were coming directly from heaven to me. I was so hungry to learn more. I took some of the small books and read them. Jamal told me I could come again if I had any questions.

As I read the books about Jesus and salvation, I felt that it was the life that I had always wanted. It wasn't just religion. I was so happy, and I started going to the library every day.

Finally, Jamal asked me if I wanted to accept the Lord Jesus as my Savior. I immediately said yes. We prayed a short prayer, and I felt so alive and happy. I wanted to run and jump and tell everyone.

I knew I had to be wise and not hasty. Jesus gives you light after a dark life. He gives you peace, love, and a big heart even though you think you're dead and don't have a heart at all.

I went home and started reading the Bible every day. I started talking to God, but not like I did before. My mind and my heart, and even my body, felt totally engaged in my prayers to God.

One day a very strange thing happened. I was walking back and forth in my room praying when, from the deepest part of me, a word came out. I know it wasn't from my mind; it was from my spirit. The word was *Father*.

I had never called God "Father." For a Muslim, this is blasphemy. I knew He was my Father, and I knew I was His son. I was so overjoyed I could hardly contain myself.

I called up Rafiq, another Christian, to tell him what I had learned. He told me that I had learned one of the greatest lessons any Christian can learn.

"It's not about religion," he said. "It's a relationship with God. He is your Father, and you are His son. Forever."

Although I couldn't go to church, I started spending all my time with the Christians. I only wanted to be with them. I felt they were my family. We were the children of God together.

Although I wasn't able to find work, I found that God always met my needs when I prayed to Him in Jesus' Name. Many times, I would be alone and unable to meet with the Christians for months, but God was with me.

Several times, God gave me dreams that have given me hope for the future. In one dream, I was holding a large fish. I shared this with a Christian named Joseph. He told me this means that God is going to use me to lead an important official to the Lord, and the official will then lead many others to the Lord as well.

I have already led others to the Lord, and we meet in secret. God also gave me new songs. The Christians said that my songs sound like the chants from the mosque. Maybe this is because I only knew those kinds of songs before. This is one of the songs:

Praise and thanks to the great Prince of Peace
Praise and thanks to the great King of Kings
Praise and thanks to my closest Friend
How I rejoice when I can hear Him
Teach me, teach me, O great Prince of Peace
Teach me, teach me, O great King of Kings Lead
me, lead me, O my closest Friend
And I rejoice when I can hear Your voice.

11
THE TESTIMONY
OF BADER

S ometimes when people tell me who to hate and who to love, I want to do the opposite. I always heard how Christians were bad people and how they didn't believe in the Koran.

There are so few Christians in my country, but we all knew them. They were friendly, and they seemed like us. They didn't dress differently from us or talk differently. They always came to our weddings and funerals. They always greeted us and wished us well during our holidays, but because of their religion, they were hated.

I didn't hate them. In fact, my best friend, Selah, was a Christian. We went to the same school, and we always played together. He didn't preach to me or talk badly about Islam. I really liked him, and I didn't think he was bad like everybody said Christians were.

Sometimes, when we were in school, our teacher would tell us that Christians were heretics and infidels and that Allah turned the Christians and Jews into pigs. Even though Selah was the only Christian in the class, he wasn't afraid to speak up. He would say, "I respect your religion and what you believe. Why must you speak about me and my family this way?"

It broke my heart to see Selah treated this way. I respected the way he defended himself even though he was alone. I wanted to be like that, but I knew I could never be a Christian. I knew I would be killed if I became a Christian.

One night, when I was sixteen-years old, I had a dream. A man on a white horse came to me. He stretched out his hand to me and said, "I am Jesus Christ. I came for you because I love you. Go to your brothers."

I woke up and was so scared. "What did the dream mean?" I wondered. What did the man mean? Who are my brothers?"

I met with Hani, a Christian man I knew, the next day. I was so afraid, but I started asking him to tell me about Jesus and the Bible. He was a real believer, and he loved Jesus so much. I could see the light in his eyes and the joy as he told me more and more about Jesus.

Even though I was scared, I felt like I had to obey the command I received in my dream. As I walked home, I was smoking a cigarette. I felt so different from before. It was almost as if I was a different person. I knew that there were many battles ahead of me.

"Why would God want me?" my mind asked. "Why did He choose to come to me? Why was I different from everyone else around me?" My family was so frustrated with me. They thought I wasn't religious enough. They wanted me to get married and get settled down like all my cousins and brothers.

I felt so restless inside. When I looked around at all the poverty and pain, I didn't think I could be like them. I wanted something more. I liked things that I knew I couldn't have, but I still wanted them. I wanted to leave the country and go to Europe or America

I wanted to marry a Christian woman and live a normal life, but it all seemed so impossible. I think that is the reason I was so different from all my peers.

Hani gave me some small books. When I got home, I started reading them, and it all made so much sense to me. I didn't think I would ever become a Christian, but I loved the books. They were so practical, and Jesus seemed so real and relatable to me.

I had another dream that night. The man on the horse came again and said, "Hani is your brother. Believe in Me because I am your Savior."

The next day, I went to Hani again and told him my dream. He was overjoyed, but I was still confused and shaken. I kept going back to Hani every day and asked him more and more questions.

Finally, while reading one of the small books that talked about how Jesus died and rose again, I realized that He was the Man in my dreams. He was the Savior. I had found the Truth. Jesus is the Truth.

I accepted Jesus in my heart. I couldn't stop smiling, and I was so happy that whole day. I kept trying to learn more and more about Jesus. I would often go to the mountains, sit alone, and read the Bible all day. There were also waterfalls near my village. I would go there to read. It felt like the water was falling into my spirit and filling me up. I could hardly contain my joy.

One day, I met another Christian man named Kris. He was from England, and we spoke English together. He taught me more and more about the Bible. I noticed that he knew much about Islam too. He told me that his father had been a Muslim, and he grew up a Muslim.

When he was a teenager, he, like me, had a vision of Jesus and knew that Jesus was the Son of God. He gave his life to the Lord and served Him in the ministry. He started teaching me about the prophesies of the end of the world.

As a Muslim, I was always intrigued by the stories we were taught about the end of the world before the Judgment Day. We were told that Jesus, whom we called Isa, would come back and judge the world. He would come to Jerusalem, "break the cross," and "kill the pig." He would say that He is a Muslim and that the world needs to become

Muslim. He would also kill the Antichrist (called "el-Diggal"), who we believed would have one eye.

Kris taught me what the Bible says. He said that Jesus would come back and judge the world. He showed me what the Bible says about the return of Christ, and he told me how many events that were prophesied are happening in our day. I was so amazed. It was so clear.

Even though my world was the same and so miserable, I had such a great hope of being with Jesus one day. I knew that I would be with Him. I was His son.

My biggest problem was that I couldn't be with the Christian brothers very much. My family was watching me and becoming suspicious of me and angry. They noticed that I didn't fast during Ramadan, and I didn't go to the mosque at all.

Someone even reported me to the police. They said I was a Christian. The police came, arrested me, and took me to the police station. They said they saw me going to church. They hit me and tried to get me to say I was or wasn't a Christian, but I wouldn't talk with them. They became frustrated and finally released me.

It was so lonely. I knew I was being watched, so I couldn't be with the Christians. In my school, we were always warned what would happen to the Muslim who becomes a Christian; and now I felt I was living that nightmare.

No one would want to marry me. No one would hire me. If someone obeyed the full counsel of the Koran, I might even be killed. In fact, if I was found out, my whole family would be persecuted even though they are Muslims. No one would want to marry my sisters. The shame was great.

I sat alone in my room and started to cry. Then I felt a hand on my head, and I looked up and saw Jesus. He said to me, "Don't be sad. Your brothers love you, and I love you."

I was so overjoyed. I knew He would be with me forever. I wanted to serve Him with all my heart. I didn't even care if someone killed me.

I started having other dreams about Jesus. Sometimes I felt like I was living in another world, not the one I was seeing around me.

There were some gun battles in my village. The Jalil and Marebi families were very powerful, and they controlled the village economy and government and fought each other all the time. Many times, innocent people got killed in the crossfire.

One December, when the mountainous region was cold and dark, a member of the Jalil family was killed by a member of the Marebi family. Even though everyone said it was an accident, an enormous battle broke out between them, and it lasted days on end. Everyone in the village was afraid to leave their homes.

A single bullet broke one of the windows in our living room. It was so cold, and the frigid wind just rushed in. We were unable to leave the house or even go near the window to fix it.

I prayed inside of myself, "Jesus, You said You would be with me and protect me. I can't stand to see my family suffer like this. Please help us. Show us Your mercy."

All of the sudden, the house became warm. The window was still broken, and the wind was still blowing, but the house was warm. I knew that I was witnessing a miracle. I went into my room and cried and thanked God.

He came to me in another dream and told me that my family and I would be safe in spite of the gunfire. He told me that He is always with me. I wrote this poem:

I have so many reasons to love Jesus
Because He makes me strong when I am weak
He gives me light during the darkness
He saved me from hell
He lifts me up when
He gives me safety during fear
He gives me hope when I am hopeless
He always keeps me warm.

I got so lonely because I couldn't be with my Christian brothers and sisters, and I decided to tell my cousin Mustafa about Jesus. He started asking many questions and then, like me, he had a dream. In the dream, he said he was in the kingdom of God, and he saw Jesus.

He started coming around all the time, and we had fellowship. I taught him how to pray and read the Bible. I taught him everything I knew. We also started singing and praying together. In spite of the fear, we always stayed together. Then his brother Rafi saw how we were so close and wanted to be with us too.

.I don't know how it happened so quickly, but I felt it was a gift from God. Both of them became Christians, and we became a little church where there was no church before. As I write this, I have tears in my eyes because I remember all that Jesus did for me and my family. I love Him so much.

12

THE TESTIMONY
OF AIDA

I was named Aida after my grandmother and was the firstborn in our family. That often doesn't mean much in a Muslim family because the glory of the family is the firstborn son. In my family, my brother Samer, who is a year younger than me, is the firstborn son.

We were born and raised in comfortable Norway. Daddy, like so many of his countrymen, made a smart escape from the violence and poverty of Mesopotamia in the late fifties. In search of a better future, he worked his way through Europe and ended up in the Land of the Midnight Sun. He quickly found work and integrated into Oslo's small but close-knit Arab community.

After finding work, he set about his second goal—finding a European wife who could help him ease through the immigration process. Daddy met a beautiful Norwegian woman named Elsa, and they fell in love.

For Mom, Daddy's religion, Islam, wasn't an issue. Secular humanism was infecting post-World War II Europe, and the farther north you travelled, the stronger its menacing grip grew.

Except for formalities, religion had pretty much been relegated to the back bin of people's lives. Marriage, of course, was one of those formalities. To get the approval of my mother's family, Daddy, did undergo a Lutheran baptism. But most everyone knew it was a sham. He was a Muslim. She was a Lutheran. That was that.

When Samer was born, Mom, in a euphoric whim, promised Daddy that Samer and I would be raised as Muslims. That didn't mean much at first. Although he is Muslim, Daddy never went to school, and he didn't know how to read or write. What he knew about Islam were the traditions, culture, and the all-important five pillars. He did teach us that God was called "Allah." He also taught us to say, "Nashkor Allah," which means "thank God."

Like Daddy, many of his cousins also feigned Christian conversion in pursuit of wedding vows and residential visas in their new Scandinavian home. Most were younger than Daddy and adapted well to their new culture.

However, my father was unswerving in his commitment to his homeland and the plight of his suffering countrymen. He spent all his time with Arabs. If he was home, he would be watching the news about his homeland.

The clash of cultures in our home became unbearable for Mom. She was culturally Scandinavian and had no intention of changing. Although he appreciated Norway and all the opportunities it afforded him, Daddy was an Arab nationalist who wouldn't back down or yield an inch. This hard-line, Arab-Islamic nationalism slowly drove a wedge between him and his wife. After a decade of marriage, she finally asked for a divorce.

Bewildered and frightened, Daddy whisked Samer and me away from Norway to his homeland. He married another woman named Sarah in his village, Abu Saiid, and left us with her. He then returned to Norway where he worked to support us.

Our stepmother was a simple, hard-working shepherd girl who took good care of us. However, after Mom's departure, I was caught in a whirlwind of life-altering events over which I had no control. I was struggling emotionally, looking for anything I could hold onto, but there was nothing; everything was moving too fast.

By the time Daddy brought us to Abu Saiid, my emotional collapse was complete. I knew how to hold up appearances in front of others, but I was devastated inside.

From the modern comforts of Europe, we were plunged into a stone-age existence. We had no electricity, no running water, and no television. We did have a radio, but the only stations were Arabic, which I didn't understand. We didn't even have a bathroom in the house; we had to use an outhouse.

Samer seemed to weather the storm better than me, but I knew he was feeling it too. He was all I had from my old life, and I wanted to be there for him. I was ten, and he was nine-years old. I had been in fifth grade and he in fourth in Norway; but because we didn't know any Arabic, we had to be put back into first grade in Abu Saiid.

We were soon doing well in our new Arabic school. We learned to speak, read, and write Arabic. Since we were older than most of our classmates, we also did well in math and other subjects, which we had already learned in Europe.

We also learned Islam, and I became very religious. I liked the stories and legends of the great heroes of the Koran. The poetic beauty of the Koran and its rhythmic recitations were so compelling.

Religion seemed like a uniter of the people in our village. People were divided over so many things, but they all came together under the banner of Islam. That was attractive to me.

In Europe, you hardly ever hear people talk about God. We saw movies about religious figures and we saw churches on the street corners, but we never heard people talking about God. It seemed that God was on off-topic, a subject discussed only in churches or homes; but in Abu Saiid, everyone talked about God. People became passionate when they talked about Islam and the prophet Mohammed.

Samer and I were like two leaves in the wind. We clung to this most stabilizing feature of village life—religion. We memorized the Koran. Culturally, we became very much like the rest of the kids in our village. Soon we were completely integrated into the culture, to the point that we had almost forgotten our European heritage and mother altogether.

After four years, Daddy brought us back to Europe. I went back to my old school. Some of the kids in school vaguely remembered me. It was comforting to be back in the world I once knew; but it had changed and I had changed.

The more I tried to fit in, then the more I felt out of place. I badly wanted a sense of identity. "Who was I?" I asked myself. "Was I Norwegian? Was I Arab?" I knew I was both, but I always felt torn as if I had to choose one or the other. In the same way that Mom and Daddy were unable to bring their two worlds together, I was also having a hard time reconciling their two worlds inside of me.

Samer seemed ecstatic about being back. As we both tried to find our way, we started growing apart. He seemed eager to forget the Old Country and just wanted to be part of European society. I found more of my sense of belonging at home. I think we both were just unable to deal with all the pain we were going through.

The one thing we both tenaciously held onto was Islam. With all the wild changes going on around me, I found more and more comfort in my religion. Even though Samer loved the European culture, he was also very devout in his commitment to Islam.

At times, Daddy would drink alcohol in the house. Samer would go in front of all Daddy's friends, take the glass of whiskey from him, and say, "The Koran says this is forbidden." Then he would spill the whiskey down the drain.

After we had been back in Norway for a year, Daddy built a new house in the Old Country. He wanted to send Sarah and her children back there to live because it was too expensive to keep them in Europe. Daddy asked Samer and me if we wanted to go back too. Samer wanted to stay in Norway, but I agreed to go with my stepmother and her two children.

Since I had many cousins and relatives in Abu Saiid, I fit in almost instantly. I went to school and did well, but I missed Daddy and Samer so much. It was enough that I hadn't seen my mother in more than six years. I didn't want to be so far away from them as well.

After a year and a half in the Old Country, I came back to Europe. Although it had only been a short time since

I had seen Samer, he had changed quite a bit. I wasn't sure what was different about him.

One day, as we were watching television, Samer looked at me and said, "I have to tell you something."

I could tell it was serious. I looked him in the eye, and he didn't say anything else. He just turned his gaze toward a small book on the coffee table. I looked at it. It was a small Bible. Then I looked back at Samer.

"The Christian religion?" I asked.

He nodded his head. "Yes, I'm a Christian, now."

"Why?" I asked him.

"I found peace in Jesus that I never had as a Muslim," he said. "Jesus is real, and He changed my life."

I tried to talk him out of it, but he was convinced. I was frustrated and scared for him. After we talked for a while, he put the book in his pocket and left the house.

I was so worried about what this would do to Daddy. So much had gone wrong in Daddy's life. He tried so hard to make things perfect for us; yet, everything seemed to fall apart around him. I didn't want to hurt him anymore by telling him about Samer, but I was also very worried that Samer would go to hell for leaving Islam.

When Daddy came home, I told him everything. I felt like Allah had sent me back to the Europe to rescue Samer from this deception. When Samer came home that night, Daddy and I tried to reason with him. He played along and said he had returned to Islam, but I knew he hadn't.

In the following weeks, we played a recording of the Koran in the house and even tried to monitor his friends to make sure he wasn't spending time with Christians. In my heart, I felt that it was hopeless. Eventually, Daddy got so angry at Samer that he kicked him out of the house. He went to live with our Mom.

I was nearing the end of my studies in gymnasium (the European equivalent of high school) by now. I kept busy with my studies and helped Daddy around the house.

At school a girl named Ava would always come around and talk with me. I liked her, but it bothered me that she spoke so much about Jesus. She would ask me to go to church with her even though she knew I was a Muslim. I never went with her, but we remained friends.

As time went on, I found myself less and less interested in religion. Even though I would never consider changing my religion like Samer, I was becoming disillusioned by what I saw in Islam.

I especially hated the way women were treated. It seemed that we had no rights. Even though Daddy was always fair with me, I couldn't accept all the things I was learning about women in Islam.

For instance, the Koran says: "Men are managers of the affairs of women because Allah has made the one superior to the other." Those words *made one superior to the other* mean that men are better than women. Not only do men have all the power, but they also have a superior nature.

In verse 34 of the Sura of the Women, the Koran even encourages husbands to beat their wives: "As for those from whom you fear disobedience, admonish them and send them to beds apart and beat them."

There was also the issue of marriage. "Why are men allowed to have four wives in Islam?" I wondered.

Mohammed was allowed to have twelve wives, and some teachers told us he had even more.

I didn't fully understand these things, but as I grew older, I grappled with them. The mere thought of these things disgusted me and infuriated me. It was so unfair and unjust.

A man is even allowed to marry a woman just to have sex with her and then divorce her with impunity. The Sura of the Women describes "pleasure" or "temporary" marriages. This is an arrangement where a man can marry a woman just for sex and then divorce her afterwards:

> And those of whom ye seek content (by marrying them), give unto them their portions as a duty. And there is no sin for you in what ye do by mutual agreement after the duty (hath been done). Lo! Allah is ever Knower, Wise.

This was in the Koran! This is in the holiest book of Islam, a book brought down to Mohammed by the Angel Gabriel, word for word from the original heavenly script.

And the *Sahih El Bakhari*, one of the most highly regarded commentaries of the prophet Mohammed, says, "I heard the Prophet (Mohammed) saying, 'Evil omen is in three things: The horse, the woman and the house.'"

"Why would Allah allow this?" I asked. I know some Muslim expositors talk about this as if it is humane, but I have seen with my own eyes what happens to so many women in the name of Islam; it is neither humane nor compassionate.

These verses felt like a bitter pill I was supposed to swallow, and I couldn't. A screaming rage inside me cried, "Why did Allah make me this way and then say all these horrible things about me?"

While I didn't want Samer's religion, I started realizing that I didn't want my religion either. I didn't want any religion. Eventually Daddy saw the battle going on inside me and felt that it would be best for me to go and be with Mom. I tried it, but it didn't work, and I eventually moved out on my own.

Samer was going to church regularly, and he tried to tell me about Jesus. But I was too angry to listen to him. I found a job at an outdoor kiosk and lived my own life.

Every now and then, I would get interested in religion again. I would try listening to the Koran and finding my way spiritually, but I couldn't accept what I was hearing. I was more intrigued by books written by American feminists like Gloria Steinem. I didn't agree with everything these writers said, but at least I felt like they saw the value of women.

During work one day, a girl gave me a small paper about a movie that was playing at the theatre. The movie was by Billy Graham. I thanked her but told her I wasn't interested.

I tried to forget about the movie; but the more I tried not to think about it, the more I thought about it. It was as if something was drawing me to go and see it, and I finally decided to go.

The movie was the story of a young American man who had never met his real father. It showed the downward spiral of his life as he traveled to Europe in search of his dad. In a strange way, his story seemed to mirror the downward spiral of my own life. Then someone told the young man some words that touched my heart: "You can't just live your whole life in rebellion to God."

The word *rebellion* just jumped out at me. That's exactly what I was doing. I was in rebellion against everybody and everything, including God. When I heard those words, I was gripped with a sense of conviction.

The movie ended with a recommended prayer:

Lord, I am a sinner. Forgive me for my sins and come into my heart. Give me a new life. I want to turn away from my sins and follow You. I believe You died for me on the cross and rose again in three days. Be with me forever. Thank You, Jesus, for dying for me.

As I prayed this, a huge burden was lifted off my heart. The pain of the years just melted away. I felt a joy, so real and tangible, that I had never known before. I could hardly wait to tell Samer.

I called him the next day. "Samer, I accepted Jesus today!"

He was overjoyed and ran all over telling all his friends. I started going to church with Samer and was overjoyed. When I was baptized in water, the pastor prophesied over me, "You will dance for joy on the hills of Jerusalem."

The joy in my heart was so great. I was growing and learning to love and relate to people again. God blessed my life so much. I had a stable job and started getting my feet firmly planted on the ground.

As time wore on, however, God started shining His light on areas of pain and rejection in my life. Seeing it and dealing with it was so painful. I often fell and suffered emotionally.

I found it hard to relate to the people in church sometimes. I so wanted to belong and be a part, but I didn't. I finally stopped going because I thought that if you're longing for chocolate, the worst place to be is a chocolate factory.

The anger and rejection I had felt as a child started rearing its head. Samer was always trying to get me to go back to church, but I didn't want anything to do with Christians or religion. I just wanted to be by myself.

Samer wrote this poem about me:

Love is more than just a longing deep inside
Is more than just the breaking of my pride
Love the Master who can hear me when I call
Who's always there to catch me when I fall,
O Love.
And though I try to break away
There can be no broken chains
Of Love,
The power that can break a heart of stone
But never just to leave it all alone
And Love,
The day that God came down to me as Man
To earth in birth, He came to understand.
O Love.
And though I try to break away
There can be no broken chain
Of Love.

I eventually moved back in with Daddy and drifted away from the church and much of what I had learned as a Christian. I never doubted Jesus, but I felt so unworthy and unwanted.

Then, as I slept one night, the Holy Spirit came. With my eyes, I saw a glorious white dove. He was flapping His wings and hovering over me. Light was emanating from Him, all around in a glorious orb. The glory was so heavy and the love was so overwhelming that I couldn't contain it; I asked Him to go away. He did—but He didn't.

He knew I couldn't contain the great love He showed me, but He wanted to show it to me anyway. He wanted me to know that I was loved with that great, immovable love. Although I couldn't accept it all at that time, I understood for the first time that I was loved with this amazing love.

Having come from a religious background, I knew so well what it meant to be afraid of God and what it meant to be under heavy condemnation and feelings of unworthiness. But the love the Holy Spirit showed me wasn't like that; it was unconditional. It wasn't based on my merit; it was based on Jesus' merit.

I learned something else too: if it's not unconditional, it's not love. I now knew that this God with whom I had to do was real. He loved me so much. I think I struggled so much at first because I didn't know if I could really trust Him. I was afraid that He too would leave me.

As the years went on, I found that I could trust Him. He was really with me, and it seemed that no matter where I would go to run from Him, He was already there waiting for me.

All my life, I had sought someone who would love me like this. Jesus is the only One who can. It wasn't about Samer anymore. It wasn't about the church or the people in it. Ultimately, I found that it was just about Jesus. He is everything to me. He came to me. And even though I did all I could to get away from Him, He never left me. He is God. He is my All in all.

13

THE TESTIMONY
OF KALI

Hello my name is Kali, This really happened to me, and I would like to share it. I was born and raised in a large city in North Africa in a very strict Sunni Muslim family. My father owns a large apartment building and converted part of the building into a mosque. All the people in that area attend that mosque.

My father is a very well-known, well-respected Muslim man, devout in his faith of Islam. Growing up Muslim, I was careful to always faithfully (salat) do my prayers and live as a good Muslim girl. I must admit that even though I prayed faithfully and obeyed the Muslim teachings, I always felt empty.

When I was a small child, it was very prestigious for families to send their children to a private Catholic school run by French foreigners. One of my family members provided the finances for me to attend this school for several years.

The school was run by nuns, and I have many, many fond memories of this school, which was filled with love and tenderness. The nuns were not permitted to teach their religion, but they daily lived their faith before us. On the last day I attended this school, I remember that I did not want to leave. I did not understand why, but I cried so hard, as if my mother had died or some terrible thing had happened.

I was transferred to a private Muslim school, and I did not like it at all. The atmosphere was very different from my loving Catholic school. I was still faithful to go through all the proper rituals as a Muslim; but the emptiness always remained. "Where is Allah?" I wondered. "Why doesn't he ever let me know that he can hear my prayers?" I began to question the Muslim faith at the age of eleven.

One day my father was sitting on the couch reading the Koran."Father," I asked him, "do you know the miracles that Jesus did? He was born of a virgin; healed the lepers; made the blind to see; and raised the dead."

Now, you must know that I have always had a strong personality. I will often speak my mind, and I am, at times, a bit rebellious.

Then I said, "Do you know what miracles Mohammed did? He married way too many women and nothing else" (Mohammed had many wives from ages nine to forty-five).

My father beat me with his belt all night for that statement. But no matter how hard he beat me, he was not able to remove the doubts I had about Islam. After the beating, I was locked in my room without any supper. A Muslim is not, under any circumstance, allowed to question Islam.

I knew the teachings about Mohammed, and I knew that his first wife was forty-five years old, a wealthy and powerful woman. They had children together, and she later died. Then Mohammed married a nine-year-old girl. This girl could not care for the children of Mohammed's first wife because she herself was a child, so he married another middle-aged wife to care for the children.

Mohammed then married many, many more women. To me, this was such a stark contrast to Jesus, who lived a holy life, without sin, and never was with a woman.

Concerning my doubts about Islam, my mother said many times over the years, "It's my fault! I never should have let you attend that Catholic school."

The harsh treatment I received from my family when I questioned Islam made we want to know even more about this Jesus of the Christian faith. It also made me want to get away from my family. I continued to observe all the Muslim customs, prayers, and fasting for Ramadan; but I still had only emptiness. I had no peace and no joy.

As an adult, I left my country to live in Europe for a couple years, and I sought to find out more about this Jesus of the Bible. One night I had a dream that was so very real. I was in the school where one goes to learn about the Koran (Masjid). I was sitting at a desk, holding a Koran in my hands, and flipping through the pages.

As I studied the words on one of the pages, I became confused. The words in the book were not those of the Koran; they were the words of the Bible. I turned to the cover of the book to make sure it was the Koran. I then looked up at the teacher (sheik) to inform him that there had been a mistake. But when I looked up at him, I did not see the sheik at all.

Jesus himself was standing before me. He looked into my eyes with such truth and boldness. He had a crown of thorns on his head, and his eyes were full of love. I knew there was something important about this dream. I was on a search for more.

Shortly after I had this dream, a wonderful woman named Sally entered my life. She knew and dearly loved this Jesus, and she had all the answers I was looking for. Sally helped me so much. She showed me truth in the Scriptures. I call her my second mom, my spiritual mother. God used her to share the scripture that led me to Jesus, to give my life to Him.

Jesus Christ, my Lord and Saviour, is now my Friend. He is not like Allah, who is cruel, unforgiving, and controlling. *Fear* is a word that describes the religion of Islam. But as I am growing in the Lord Jesus Christ, I am finding peace in the midst of every storm. Jesus Christ is my Friend and Comrade. He speaks to me through His words, the Bible, and His Spirit. We have a relationship like that of a loving father and a daughter.

I did not leave Islam, the religion, to join another religion, Christianity; rather, I left Islam and all religious affiliations to become a child of the most High God and King, Jesus our Creator. I am His daughter and princess.

THE EPILOGUE

What you have just read is true and accurate in every detail except the location of the miracles and the names of those involved in the miracles. I changed the names to protect those involved, along with their families.

As you can see through these true stories that God has a special place in His heart for Muslims. Try the experiment and call out to the God of the Universe. The Bible is very clear in that if we come to Him with a pure honest heart and ask and seek Him for the truth He will answer and reveal the truth, because of His love for all mankind, He is good to His promise of answering.

My prayer for you is this that you will give God a chance in your life. If Jesus (Isa) is the *only* way to the God of the Universe, as the Holy Bible states He is, all you need to do is come talk to Him from your heart. Your words don't have to be exact or flowery, just an open and honest prayer to the God of the Universe. Say something like this;

> God of Abraham, reveal to me the truth any way You want. You know my heart better than I know it, so speak to me through any means You wish. I will accept Your message, whether it is by a dream, vision, visitation, or miracle. I just want to know the truth. Amen.

How to Say Yes to God

If you know that Jesus is real and want to accept Him into your heart, the precise words you use to commit yourself to Him are not important. He knows the intentions of your heart. If you are unsure of what to pray, this might help you put it into words:

> Jesus, I want to know You. I want You to come into my life. Thank You for dying on the cross for the forgiveness of my sin so that I can be fully accepted by You. Only You can give me the power to change and become the person You created me to be. Thank You for forgiving me and giving me eternal life with God. I now turn away from all my sinfulness, please bring to me the PEACE as you promised those who accept you. I give my life to You. Please do with it as You wish. Amen.
>
> If you said that prayer from your heart and really meant it then here is what the Holy Bible says is true about you. You have BECOME a child of Almighty God your Heavenly Father.

My Dear Child,

You may not know me, but I know everything about you. Psalm 139:1

I know when you sit down and when you rise up. Psalm 139:2

I am familiar with all your ways. Psalm 139:3

Even the very hairs on your head are numbered.

Matthew 10:29-31 For you were made in my image.

Genesis 1:27 In me you live and move and have your being. Acts 17:28

For you are my offspring. Acts 17:28

I knew you even before you were conceived. Jeremiah 1:4-5

I chose you when I planned creation. Ephesians 1:11-1

You were not a mistake, for all your days are written in my book. Psalm 139:15-16

I determined the exact time of your birth and where you would live. Acts 17:26

You are fearfully and wonderfully made. Psalm 139:14

I knit you together in your mother's womb. Psalm 139:13

And brought you forth on the day you were born. Psalm 71:6

I have been misrepresented by those who don't know me. John 8:41-44

I am not distant and angry, but am the complete expression of love. 1 John 4:16

And it is my desire to lavish my love on you. 1 John 3:1

Simply because you are my child and I am your Father. 1 John 3:1

I offer you more than your earthly father ever could. Matthew 7:1

For I am the perfect father. Matthew 5:48

Every good gift that you receive comes from my hand. James 1:17

For I am your provider and I meet all your needs. Matthew 6:31-33

My plan for your future has always been filled with hope. Jeremiah 29:11

Because I love you with an everlasting love. Jeremiah 31:3

My thoughts toward you are countless as the sand on the seashore. Psalms 139:17-18

And I rejoice over you with singing. Zephaniah 3:17

I will never stop doing good to you. Jeremiah 32:40

For you are my treasured possession. Exodus 19:5

I desire to establish you with all my heart and all my soul. Jeremiah 32:41

And I want to show you great and marvelous things. Jeremiah 33:3

If you seek me with all your heart, you will find me. Deuteronomy 4:29

Delight in me and I will give you the desires of your heart. Psalm 37:4

For it is I who gave you those desires. Philippians 2:13

I am able to do more for you than you could possibly imagine. Ephesians 3:20

For I am your greatest encourager. 2 Thessalonians 2:16-17

I am also the Father who comforts you in all your troubles. 2 Corinthians 1:3-4

When you are brokenhearted, I am close to you. Psalm 34:18

As a shepherd carries a lamb, I have carried you close to my heart. Isaiah 40:1

One day I will wipe away every tear from your eyes. Revelation 21:3-4

And I'll take away all the pain you have suffered on this earth. Revelation 21:3-

I am your Father, and I love you even as I love my son, Jesus. John 17:23

For in Jesus, my love for you is revealed. John 17:26

He is the exact representation of my being. Hebrews 1:3

He came to demonstrate that I am for you, not against you. Romans 8:31

And to tell you that I am not counting your sins. 2 Corinthians 5:18-19

Jesus died so that you and I could be reconciled. 2 Corinthians 5:18-19

His death was the ultimate expression of my love for you. 1 John 4:10

I gave up everything I loved that I might gain your love. Romans 8:31-32

If you receive the gift of my son Jesus, you receive me. 1 John 2:23

And nothing will ever separate you from my love again. Romans 8:38-39

Come home and I'll throw the biggest party heaven has ever seen. Luke 15:7

I have always been Father, and will always be Father. Ephesians 3:14-15

My question is…Will you be my child? John 1:12-13

I am waiting for you. Luke 15:11-32

Love, Your Father

Almighty God

You may e-mail the compiler of these stories at:
aliabdelmasih@yahoo.com

You may order books online at
www.outofdarknessintolight.com
or
www.jesusdied4mohamed2.com

You may also order the books through the printer-publisher
by sending $10.00 + $1.00 to:

MGB Printing Services Inc.
10276 East Point Douglas Rd S.
Cottage Grove, MN 55016
mgbprinting@gmail.com

For more information and a discount
please call 651-459-4220 to order in bulk.